walks of the Mornington Peninsula

Ken Martin

Publishing

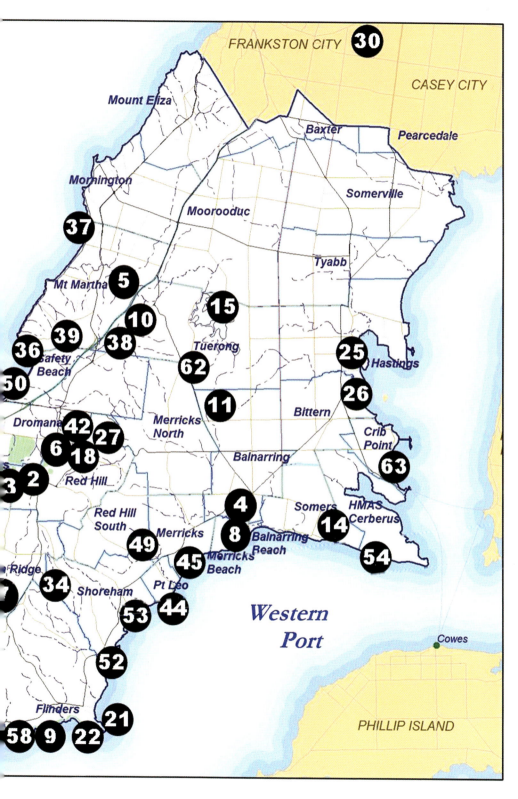

GENERAL INFORMATION

This book has been compiled by walking enthusiasts to enable others to enjoy the beautiful natural environment of the Mornington Peninsula. All information is as accurate as possible, but no responsibility can be accepted for difficulties encountered. Track conditions, signage and vegetation will most likely change over time so be flexible and use your judgement and discretion as required.

© Ken Martin. 2018.

Bas Publishing Pty Ltd
PO Box 335
Dromana Vic 3936

www.baspublishing.com.au
mail@baspublishing.com.au

Also by the same author:

Walks of the Surf Coast 2011
Walks of the Shipwreck Coast and Volcano Country 2010
Walks of King Island 2001, 2009
Walks of Flinders Island 1999, 2001, 2008
Walks of the Mornington Peninsula 2000, 2003, 2005, 2007, 2008, 2012, 2015, 2018
The Walks of Port Campbell and the Shipwreck Coast 2000, 2001
The Walks of the Volcano Country 2001, 2005
The Walks of Killiecrankie and Environs 1997
The Walks of King Island 2001, 2009

This book is copyright. Apart from fair dealing for the purposes of private study, research, criticism or review, as permitted under the Copyright Act, no part may be reproduced by any process without written permission of the publisher.

National Library of Australia Cataloguing-in-Publication entry

Author: Martin, Ken.

Title: Walks of the Mornington Peninsula

ISBN: 9781921496165 (pbk)

Subjects: Hiking--Victoria--Mornington Peninsula--Guidebooks. Mornington Peninsula (Vic.)--Guidebooks.

Dewey Number: 919.452

Images by Ken Martin
Maps by Rocco Russo
Front Cover Image: Rye Jetty and Arthurs Seat
Back Cover Image: Cape Schanck Lighthouse

Layout and Design: Ben Graham

ABORIGINAL TRADITIONAL OWNERS

We acknowledge the Aboriginal Traditional Owners of Victoria - including its parks and reserves. Through their cultural traditions, Aboriginal people maintain their connection to their ancestral lands and waters. We further recognize the Boonwurrung/Bunerong people as the traditional custodians of the land.

CODE RED FIRE DANGER RATING DAYS

Visit the Parks Victoria website: www.parkweb.vic.gov.au

Note: On days of **Code Red Fire Danger** all state forests and forest parks will be closed for public safety.

Parks Victoria have released a pamphlet titled: 'Park and Forest Closures on Code Red Fire Danger Rating days.' Nov. 2010 which outlines your responsibilities and guidance regarding weather forecasts, etc. on fire danger days.

VISITOR INFORMATION CENTRES

The centres listed below offer a wealth of information on accommodation and attractions, galleries and boutique wineries, beaches through to maps and golf courses as well as wildlife adventures and marine experiences.

DROMANA Peninsula Visitor Information Centre, 359B Point Nepean Road, Dromana - Tel: 03 5987 3078

FRANKSTON Frankston Visitor Information Centre, Pier Promenade, Frankston Waterfront, Frankston - Tel: 1300 322 842

HASTINGS Western Port Tourist Information Centre, Westhaven Boat Harbour, Hastings - Tel: 03 5979 0404 MORNINGTON

MORNINGTON Information Centre, 2 Main Street, Mornington - Tel: 03 5975 1644

SORRENTO Sorrento Visitor Information, St Aubins Way, Sorrento - Tel: 03 5984 1478

CONTENTS

INTRODUCTION 9
WHY WALK? 12
HIKING GEAR AND OTHER ESSENTIALS 17
SUGGESTED LIST OF EQUIPMENT 18
1. ARTHURS SEAT TO BROWNS ROAD 20
2. ARTHURS SEAT STATE PARK TO EATONS CUTTING 25
3. ARTHURS SEAT – THE FRIENDS TRACK 28
4. BALBIROOROO WETLANDS BALNARRING 31
5. BALCOMBE ESTUARY NATURE PARK TRAIL 34
6. BALD HILL NATURE CONSERVATION RESERVE 38
7. BALDRY CROSSING CIRCUIT 41
8. BALNARRING BEACH TO MERRICKS CREEK 45
9. BLOW HOLE TRACK FLINDERS 48
10. BRIARS WETLANDS AND WOODLANDS RESERVE 51
11. BUCKLEY NATURE CONSERVATION RESERVE 55
12. CAPE SCHANCK LIGHTHOUSE AND BUSHRANGERS BAY 58
13. CHINAMANS CREEK, WEST ROSEBUD TO RYE 64
14. COOLART WETLANDS AND HOMESTEAD 68
15. DEVILBEND RESERVOIR 72
16. DROMANA TO ARTHURS SEAT 75
17. DROMANA, McCRAE LIGHTHOUSE AND ROSEBUD 79
18. EATONS CUTTING CIRCUIT 83
19. FINGAL BEACH AND SELWYN FAULT 85
20. FINGAL PICNIC AREA AND BEACH CIRCUIT 88
21. FLINDERS JETTY TO WEST HEAD 92
22. FLINDERS OCEAN BEACH WALK 96
23. FLINDERS TO CAPE SCHANCK 99
24. GUNNAMATTA TO BOAGS ROCKS 103
25. HASTING FORESHORE RESERVE 107
26. JACKS BEACH RESERVE TO HASTINGS 110
27. KANGERONG NATURE CONSERVATION RESERVE 113
28. KINGS FALLS 115
29. KOONYA OCEAN BEACH TO SORRENTO OCEAN BEACH 118

30. LANGWARRIN FLORA AND FAUNA RESERVE 121
31. LATROBE RESERVE, DROMANA 125
32. LONG POINT, CAPE SCHANCK 128
33. MAIN CREEK WALK 132
34. MAIN RIDGE NATURE CONSERVATION RESERVE.................. 134
35. MAIN RIDGE TO CAPE SCHANCK 137
36. MARTHA POINT, PEBBLE BEACH, MT MARTHA 142
37. MORNINGTON TO MT MARTHA CLIFFTOP WALK.................. 146
38. MT MARTHA COMMUNITY FOREST.. 150
39. MT MARTHA PARK... 153
40. NUMBER 16 TO KOONYA OCEAN BEACH 156
41. NUMBER 16 TO RYE OCEAN BEACH... 160
42. OT DAM AND ARTHURS SEAT STATE PARK 164
43. PENINSULA GARDENS BUSHLAND RESERVE, ROSEBUD........ 167
44. POINT LEO 171
45. POINT LEO TO BALNARRING BEACH 174
46. POINT NEPEAN NATIONAL PARK 177
47. PORTSEA OCEAN BEACH TO LONDON BRIDGE 186
48. PORTSEA TO SORRENTO ARTISTS TRAIL............................... 191
49. RED HILL TO MERRICKS TRAIL 195
50. SAFETY BEACH TO DROMANA AND ANTHONY'S NOSE........ 198
51. SEAWINDS TO SEAMIST DRIVE ARTHURS SEAT 202
52. SHOREHAM TO FLINDERS.. 205
53. SHOREHAM TO POINT LEO 210
54. SOMERS TO SANDY POINT... 214
55. SORRENTO OCEAN BEACH AND ROCKPOOLS 218
56. SORRENTO TO BLAIRGOWRIE.. 221
57. STAR WALK METEORS AND SATELLITES ALIVE..................... 225
58. TEA TREE CREEK FLINDERS 228
59. TOOTGAROOK WETLANDS.. 231
60. WATERFALL CREEK BUSHLAND RESERVE.............................. 234
61. WHITECLIFFS, RYE TO BLAIRGOWRIE 238
62. WOODS RESERVE.. 243
63. WOOLLEYS BEACH CRIB POINT... 246
ABOUT THE AUTHOR.. 249
ALSO AVAILABLE.. 251
REFERENCES AND RESOURCES.. 253
USEFUL WEBSITES 254

INTRODUCTION

Walking on the Mornington Peninsula

It is said that Victoria is a compact state, one that offers a wide range of environments and climatic zones within a few hundred kilometres. As well, there is the relatively high density of population. Lots of towns and cities in relative close proximity to one another. Here on the Mornington Peninsula we have a tremendous range of natural environments that can be experienced within a few short kilometres.

Consider this diversity:

The desert like sand dunes of the ocean beaches around Gunnamatta. The subtropical rainforests of Greens Bush and the open savannah forests of Woods Reserve. The extensive mangroves between Jacks Beach and Hastings. What about the wild power of the rugged ocean coastline lined with cliffs, volcanic in origin and surf pounding on the shoreline. The Blow Hole Track at Flinders. Prolific wetlands at Coolart and The Briars with their attendant water bird populations. A history of defence and fortifications at Point Nepean from World War I and World War II and the saga of the Quarantine Station and the cemetery nearby. Paper bark trees lining Balcombe Creek, are very manner reminiscent of parts of King Island. Martha Point with its distinctive orange coloured rocks is almost identical to some of the Flinders Island coastline, 300 kilometres to the southeast.

There is the peninsula at play:

Walk past colourful boat sheds of all sizes and descriptions which line Port Phillip Bay. There are the ocean and bay lifesaving clubs which you will pass on your coastal walks, making safe the seaside environment for visitors and locals alike. And then there is a vulcanism to be seen on West Head at Flinders. Hexagonal columns of basalt and a volcanic plug at Pulpit Rock, Cape Schanck. A sandy and scrubby section of the Langwarrin Flora and Fauna Reserve reminds me of the Little Desert National Park, hundreds of kilometres to the north-west of the State. The tide exposed rock platforms of the Nepean National Park always impress with the diversity of life and the tenacity with which the bubble weed and bull kelp anchor themselves to the bedrock.

Victoria, indeed, is a very compact state with much to see within its boundaries. The Mornington Peninsula is perhaps a small reflection of its larger geographical partner. The challenge then is to go and explore these areas, perhaps visiting two or more locations in the day, if time permits. It's okay to read about and see all the concern for the environment in the media but unless we physically get out and see for ourselves we are merely armchair environmentalists. Many of the walks described in the book are of short duration. They are not necessarily too taxing of your effort nor too demanding of your time. We often talk of 'Planet Earth.' Now is the time not only to see and experience it for ourselves but also to bring along our families and friends so that we can all enjoy the magnificent Mornington Peninsula environment.

WARNING

- Walking along ocean beaches is always challenging and it can allow a full appreciation of nature's untamed power. However, any ocean coastline subject to surf or ocean waves can present a real and present danger to walkers. Large waves, sometimes nearly **twice the height** of the average wave height or surf that you experience can crash onto the coast, literally without warning. Scientists and oceanographers tell us these 'rogue' or 'freak' waves **will occur** every 2 to 3 hours, perhaps around every 1000th wave. The message is clear. Do not take risks along any ocean beaches on the Mornington Peninsula or elsewhere. Arrive alive. (Source: Wind Waves and Weather. Victorian Waters. Bureau of Meteorology.) Please heed all advisory signs.

WHY WALK?

Walking has become extremely fashionable. With low carbon emissions and keeping ourselves away from the computer screen, it is the ultimate 'all green' activity. As well as the physical benefits of keeping active, walking is mentally relaxing and it can rejuvenate your motivation for life. Walking with friends or in groups can further develop friendships and increase your social network. Walking gives you some quiet time and with less stimulus it can be like a meditation.

Did you realize that fitness experts claim a fast walking pace uses more energy than a slow jog? Walking is an excellent medium with which to develop cardiovascular fitness. Improved cardiovascular fitness can reduce blood pressure, major muscle groups are exercised and there is the potential for long term walking and general exercise to lead to a reduction in your basal heart rate. Medical scientists say that exercise can also keep blood sugar levels in check too.

A good distance hike or walk can be challenging because of the distance involved as well as the degree of difficulty, be it ascending terrain or the goal of covering considerable distances over a set time frame. And a solid nights' sleep after a big walk is satisfying in its own right, too.

New walking venues have the potential to offer the bushwalker a smorgasbord of visual delights: from observing the tiniest flower and the smallest lichen to grand panoramas: perhaps a rainbow cast against the backdrop of a wild ocean or a mist covered mountain. The sighting of a migratory bird that has perhaps travelled half a world to be here. There is a never-ending kaleidoscope of images perhaps as simple as the setting sun or a rain cloud with its attendant virga rain tails.

New scenery is a real plus: there is the interest of a new and remote location, perhaps seldom visited by people. The allure of shore bird calls and the wind in the trees. Spotting wildlife such as a possum, kangaroo or wallaby can have its own rewards.

Walking is good for the environment. Your eco footprint will be low with any walking activity. Walking is probably one of the lowest forms of human activity in carbon emissions, perhaps only bettered by sitting and sleeping. We won't count the environmental 'cost' of driving to your walking destination.

Improved fitness can bolster both self-esteem and self-confidence and a regular programme of daily exercise, particularly walking, should be part of everyone's daily routine to bolster good well-being. The ancient Greeks had a concept they termed *Euexia* (Pronounced you-ex-eeya) which meant "good health" or "good habit of body". Perhaps we need to return to this simple and all-encompassing concept. We 'can use it or lose it' is an often-cited expression these days. All we have to do is 'keep on walking'.

Have you ever thought about getting up earlier to make time for a walk? Whether you are a visitor on holidays, a local who has yet to visit all the walking locations in your area or perhaps you are on a business trip to the area, the challenge goes out – walk. I endeavour to rise early, particularly in the holidays, to explore the surrounding environment. Walking pre-dawn and watching a sunrise is a special experience. Walking on a spectacular sunset is likewise a special event. I ate one summers' evening I chanced to see Venus in the far west, shining in an orange shrouded sky with wispy cirrus clouds completing the picture.

Visitors, holiday makers and residents alike will find the best way to experience all that an area has to offer is to walk and take in the sights and sounds, the vegetation and the weather of a particular location. On offer then, in this collection of walks, is the incentive to get into the 'great outdoors'. Perhaps Wordsworth best summed up the concept when he said: 'An eye to perceive and a heart to enjoy.'

There has been a huge amount of research conducted into the benefits of walking. Like any cardio-vascular exercise program walking can reduce the risk of coronary disease and stroke as well as lowering blood pressure. Cholesterol levels can also be reduced and further studies point to a lift in bone density for participants of that particular study. Even back pain, which is said to afflict up to seventy per cent of the population at various stages of their lives, can be better managed and even reduced in severity. As is stated with any new exercise program, consult your general practitioner before undertaking any new program of vigorous exercise, especially if you have been leading a sedentary lifestyle.

Mark Fenton in his article 'Jump off a Bridge' makes persuasive arguments for daily walking which include helping you maintain a healthy weight, improving muscle tone and clearing your head.

The U.S. Surgeon General cites that 30 minutes of walking per day can reduce your risk of chronic disease and research also confirms that regular walkers live longer, more independent lives. Perhaps you are unable to do a 'bushwalk' every day. Most of us have families to consider and the day-to-day routine of work and household duties. Certainly we can all make some time every day to get in a walk before work, at lunchtime or at the end of the day. I caught up with one of my primary school buddies from many years ago and he ended up in a very high powered job in Canberra, up to 24/7 yet he always made time to have a lunchtime walk and he made sure that the mobile was left in the office for this regular 'indulgence.' What a great way to look after yourself. I've been a long time practitioner of the 'lunchtime break' at work. But rather than sit around at the office or staff room I endeavour to get out and walk in the winter and, weather permitting, swim over the summer months. I maintain that I can walk back into the office immediately after lunch and feel almost as fresh and as mentally alert as I was at 9 am for the start of the working day. While my lunchtime walks are usually over the same patch of ground, this is still a very useful and beneficial exercise routine. Once a week I team up with a few work buddies for a 45 minute power walk. This is also a great motivator. Not only do we talk our 'heads off' about any and everything, we also all feel pumped at the end of the 'workout' ready to hit the afternoon shift with gusto.

The benefits of walking were also cited in a report by the British Government in 2008. The findings were offered on the basis of recommendations from over 400 specialists and specifically, being active: 'just (taking) a daily stroll will make you feel good and maintain mobility and fitness.'

I like to think that a regular daily exercise regime, albeit short at times, better prepares you for the longer haul walks that can be undertaken on a weekend or after work during the daylight saving hours. Simply keeping fit can give you the confidence to tackle what, on paper, can seem a long or arduous distance, but once you have the kilometres under your belt it is surprising how the kilometres can add up and all of a sudden you may have tackled 10 or 20 kilometres without really working up too much of a sweat.

Kristina Hurrell in her excellent article entitled 'Take a Hike' alludes to the higher gains on offer to dedicated walkers. Hiking for 'health, happiness and harmony' may seem like a big ask. But consider that the endorphin rush usually associated with runners is available to serious walkers for less strenuous effort than runners who pound the pavement. Hiking, Hurrell asserts, can be a thrill for the senses and if you've got some worries walking is certainly a useful tool for combating stress. I've maintained for some time that walking solo can be like a meditation. There is time to reflect, to put matters into perspective and to simply think about issues and the alternatives that may be available. Your quality of life can improve with regular walking. The 'I can-do-it' self-confidence that is generated with a serious walk has got to be a big plus for this sport! By walking tall and walking in an assertive manner, your self-confidence and self-esteem can rise quickly. I know that when I'm pacing myself at up to five and seven kilometres per hour (on suitable walking tracks) the surge in adrenalin and a real feeling of power become apparent. The feeling of getting some kilometres under your feet and reaching a distant point or objective is always a positive and leads to a real feeling of satisfaction and contentment.

Frederick Nietzsche, the German philosopher wrote that: 'All great thoughts are conceived while walking'. Having some quiet time to spend with your own thoughts can be very productive and a good walk can be just the medium to keep you away from household and work distractions so that you can devote time to the issue or problem at hand.

And what about Hippocrates, the ancient Greek philosopher who said over 2000 years ago that "Walking is man's best medicine."

Walking with good friends and with an interesting venue is also said to reduce depression and anxiety. A regular walking program may also improve your coordination and reflexes. You may be less likely to fall and suffer leg or hand fractures because your bones are stronger and your reflexes are sharper and more responsive. Similarly, you may be less likely to sustain any injury because your joints have a better range of motion and the muscles are more flexible.

If there was ever a time to go and walk it is now.

HIKING GEAR AND OTHER ESSENTIALS

Take your hiking seriously. Let someone know of your intentions. Do not walk over wet rocks. Take special care when walking along the ocean coastline and watch out for large waves! There is an excellent brochure on 'Shore Safety' which details many of the hazards which can be encountered on the coast. See www.ga.gov.au In 2010 the New South Wales coastline had claimed something in the order of 23 citizens in 24 months, with 5 people perishing in a single incident! The message is very clear. Be extremely cautious if you are walking along any coastal region near the waters' edge.

Be prepared for the worst but walk when conditions are optimal. Here's a list of some of my preferred hiking items. Obviously, if you're doing a short walk along a clearly marked track that you are familiar with, you'll include just a few of the items below. For a half day's walk in unfamiliar terrain with a number of people in your group, it is certainly prudent to take gear sufficient for most eventualities.

We should remember that a Victorian cabinet minister who was lost overnight in less than optimal conditions was fortunate to be found relatively unscathed. Other walkers have been less fortunate. A solo walker was lost for 3 days some years ago, within a few kilometres of the road and beaches! Another hiker in Tasmania did not return from a solo expedition. A mobile phone and an EPIRB or PLB are good investments. The message is clear. Do not walk alone. Be very well prepared. Basic navigation skills and good map (with a waterproof cover) are also essential. Check out the weather radar and district forecast for your area before undertaking any extended or longer walks. Even load your mobile phone with the weather radar site for Melbourne! Play it safe. Start with a walk that will be well within the capabilities of everyone in your group. In 2011, I was amazed to see three 'walkers', one of which had to be air-lifted to safety near Martha Point, without any equipment, water, daypack or the like. Some would say they were completely unprepared, particularly as the day was warm and humid and they appeared to have no fluid refreshments whatsoever.

A first aid kit is also an essential equipment item for any serious walker. There are many commercially available kits but you can also build up your own first aid kit with items from your home medicine cabinet. A first aid course is also a very worthwhile investment. Many workplaces now offer Level II First Aid courses so take the initiative and get yourself trained. First aid training is also provided by the Red Cross www.redcross.org.au and St. Johns www.stjohn.org.au as well as many private providers.

SUGGESTED LIST OF EQUIPMENT

- Beany or sun hat
- Binoculars
- Compass or iPhone equivalent
- **Day pack**
- **First aid kit** with roller bandages, steri-strips, etc
- Food, snacks
- Hike footwear, lightweight, **good tread** for rock hopping
- LED Torch or headlamp
- **Maps** 1:100 000 or 1:25 000 series,
- Matches
- **Melways** or similar, GPS navigational guide or SuperPages, Peninsula
- **Mobile phone**, digitized maps
- Navman - GPS driven pedometer
- Notebook, pencil and tide guide

Rye Ocean Beach.

- PFD (compact), with cartridge, yoke type, for serious coastal walking
- PLB (Personal Locator Beacon) or EPIRB,
- **Raincoat**, shorts and long strides
- Rope/line 3-4 mm .. guys for your tarp! Tent pegs
- Small poly tarp 2m x 2m A great emergency shelter and ground sheet
- UV cream, sunglasses, zinc cream
- **Walking pole** or poles
- **WATER** minimum 2 litres per person

ARTHURS SEAT TO BROWNS ROAD

Try a section of the Two Bays Walk from the majestic Arthurs Seat summit and the impressive Seawinds gardens through forested and suburban precincts. Great views of Port Phillip Bay and the southern Mornington Peninsula. This is part of the renowned 'Two Bays Walk'.

Start	Seawinds carpark, Arthurs Seat
Distance	7.2 kms
Time	2+ hours
Grade	Medium, mainly downhill
Map	Melways 159 D12, 171 D1
When	Almost anytime. Avoid on Code Red Days
Suggestion	Car pickup at Browns Road

Before commencing your 'Two Bays' trek you may like to investigate the William Ricketts sculptures, found within the Seawinds gardens and approximately 240 metres from carpark. The excellent facilities at Seawinds include an amenities block, barbecues, picnic shelters, tank water, tables and seats. A roofed shelter contains maps of the walking tracks and other interesting details on the area.

The area is very well maintained with open space that would be suitable for families with young children who need an area to run around.

At the northern lookout, which is highly recommended, at just over 300 metres elevation, there are standout views of Port Phillip Bay, the

Arthurs Seat lookout at Seawinds.

narrowing of the peninsula towards Port Phillip Heads and the Otways in the distance.

This lookout also has signage highlighting the geological formation of Port Phillip Bay.

The walking track from Arthurs Seat and the Seawinds picnic is well signposted. It starts as a wide gravel track and winds its way into forested path. In late summer, on a superb, sunny day, common brown butterflies were in profusion along parts of this track. The wildflowers had obviously taken advantage of the summer rains to offer a display of colour and delicacy. As you walk along the track towards Seamists Drive, signage highlights the T. C. McKellar Reserve, which contains significant remnant vegetation. Another sign highlights the issue of cinnamon fungus. The track starts to deteriorate into a narrower, earthen path which negotiates some tree roots, and large stone and timber steps. Take time on your walk to stop and listen for the sounds of bird life. Birds aren't always visible but they can certainly make their presence heard.

Eventually you will arrive at four way junction which heads left to Seamists Drive, to King's Waterfall, and to McLarens Dam. You need to take the track to McLelland Dam. King's waterfall is 850 metres distant and this feature could be included on this walk or left for investigation at another time. Walking is now on a gravelled four-wheel-drive management track. With more open terrain and descending past emergency marker ART 500, there are superb views towards Point Nepean and Bass Strait. In late summer the Spirit of Tasmania, running on a daytime schedule, was clearly visible with its red hull and white superstructure, as it made its way through the heads. This is where a pair of compact binoculars can be useful. The gravel four-wheel-drive track becomes steeper and my suggestion is to walk on the grass shoulder for a better grip as the gravel is somewhat loose and slippery in parts.

The track turns into a more southerly direction and on this clear day there were three yachts visible out in Bass Strait. As well, a containership could be seen further out to sea. As you descend towards suburbia and the freeway, urban traffic noise becomes quite apparent. You have left the relative quiet of the forested Arthurs Seat State Park. As you approach another four-way Junction signage indicates Waterfall Gully Road at 700 metres. There is a rusted water tank nearby. At this point you are at an elevation of 120 metres having made a descent from around 300 metres at the top of Arthurs Seat. Approaching McLaren Dam the four wheel drive track becomes very steep and needs some caution with its loose gravel. Walking poles could be a decided advantage here. Signage as you approach the dam is somewhat limited. Keep bearing roughly straight ahead after a slight dog leg in the track which now takes you across the dam wall. Keep a map handy for ready reference, preferably in a plastic pouch. After the wet summer season of 2011 the dam spillway was still discharging water. This was a marked

McLaren's Dam.

contrast to the many dry summers we had experienced in recent years. Look out for ducks in the dam.

Very shortly you arrive at Waterfall Gully Road. There is a Parks Victoria gate, fencing and signage. Directions indicate that you walk down the road into Goolgowrie Road, following the Two Bays walking markers. You are now passing suburban streets and residential development. Turn into Avalon Street and enter the well marked reserve. It is approximately 2.5 kilometres to Browns Rd. This reserve is a delightful patch of forest, well maintained, with an extensive boardwalk of over 100 metres. The dense vegetation here includes kangaroo paw ferns, fishbone ferns and another fern I could not identify. After the boardwalk there is a well formed gravel track which terminates at a children's playground. Follow the road to the right until you reach Duells Road and then turn left. Follow this sealed road which turns to gravel. When this road terminates you will notice the walking track on your right hand side. This is a bush walking track which obviously has far less use. It descends past a memorial cairn dedicated to a local naturalist and bushwalker. The track then passes through a paper bark forest, and is somewhat reminiscent of King Island paper bark forests. There are some small board walks to negotiate and soon you are walking through a very impressive grass tree forest, some with spears and with healthy stands of eucalyptus. You are now climbing towards Browns Road and your final destination. The Two Bays Track you have just traversed meets Browns Road directly opposite Hyslops Road where there is limited parking, if required.

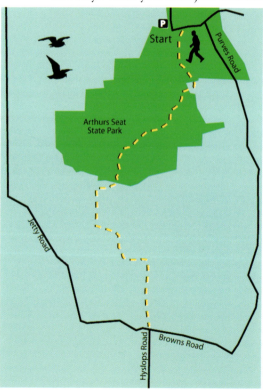

At this point phone for your vehicle pickup or use the shuttle car to return to the start of this walk.

ARTHURS SEAT STATE PARK TO EATONS CUTTING

This challenging walk passes one of the most picturesque 'lakes' on the peninsula, perched high on the Arthurs Seat hill. Most walkers are surprised to see this tranquil gem. As well there is the option to extend the walk and complete the Eatons Cutting circuit walk.

Start	Arthurs Seat Road, 250 metres west of Main Creek Road
Distance	6 kilometres
Time	2+ hours
Grade	Medium
Maps	Melways: Map 190 A2
When	Anytime

This walk, initially well-signposted, starts about 250 metres west of the Arthurs Seat Road and Main Creek Road intersection. Head out along the track, a 4WD management vehicle road, to the OT Dam, approximately 1.1 kilometres away. At the first opportunity, where a sign indicates the OT Dam is 500 metres, take the right hand four-wheel-drive track which descends towards the OT Dam. This track is a short-cut but you can also take the main track to the dam which is slightly longer. Note that you will pass the Friends Track (see walk number 3) which is on your left.

On my recent early morning walk in this area much bird life was in evidence, particularly a small flock noisy Rosellas. At around 8 a.m. the forest looked of very fresh after overnight rain, the sun was filtering

Creek at Arthurs Seat State Park.

through the trees and illuminating some cobwebs which were nearby. Note: the black trunks of some of the eucalyptus trees in this vicinity are the result of previous wildfire. Approach another T intersection and follow the left hand main four-wheel-drive track which now approaches the south eastern end of the OT Dam.

Walk over a small bridge and spillway. Take time to investigate the shoreline of this very picturesque dam, a former campsite and water supply for a jam making industry many years ago. There is a treated pine barrier which leads over the eastern dam wall. After investigating the dam you will take the smaller and more insignificant track towards the northeast. The early morning suns rays highlight the great display of forest vegetation which abounds in this area.

Look for the kangaroo paw fern below the north eastern dam wall and especially the long needled Casuarina trees nearby. Walking in an anticlockwise direction around the dam, just beyond the dam wall are some steps which rise to give views of the northern part of this dam

After taking in the tranquillity of this 'magic' dam, head out for Eatons Cutting, take the track immediately opposite the bridge over the spill way. The track here is of lower grade and more like a true bush walking track, one person in width, quite a change from the wide 4WD track.

You will cross a very small creek with some maiden hair fern along its banks. On my last visit I had to negotiate two fallen trees and then another steep descent to a second small creek. As well there are some fish bone ferns and a solitary tree fern. The ascent towards Eatons Cutting Road is medium to hard in places and you pass a small dam on your right. When you meet the four-wheel-drive track take the right hand route. At another fork in the track take the right hand option and the stay on the wider four-wheel-drive track. Before long your four-wheel-drive track will intersect with the Eatons Cutting Road. From here continue to the right, passing a fibro holiday dwelling on your left. You will come to a management gate and you have now arrived at Lookout Road where it is apparent that you are now in a residential area.

The choices from here are as follows.

1. Walk to Eatons Cutting Lookout. (See walk no 18.)

2. Follow the road out towards Arthurs Seat Road then walk approximately two kilometres on the horse trail back to the car parking area.

or

3. Retrace your steps via OT Dam.

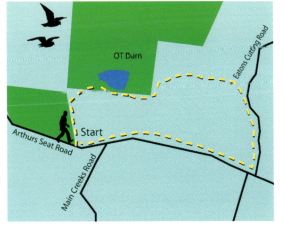

ARTHURS SEAT – THE FRIENDS TRACK

A relaxing and pleasant walk through impressive stands of vegetation and a stone ruin all add interest to this delightful Arthurs Seat trek. Easy grades with plenty of twists and turns, this shorter walk may also appeal to younger children in your walking group.

Start	OT Track, Arthurs Seat Road.
Distance	3 kilometres return
Time	Under 1 hour return
Grade	Easy
Maps	Melways: Map 171 K2
When	Anytime except Code Red days

Start this walk by heading out for the OT Dam. Just over half a kilometre from the start of your walk, on your right, is the Friends Track. This track is signposted and initially follows a four-wheel-drive track but you will need to navigate yourself onto the walking path from the four-wheel-drive track which is not signposted. This signage indicates Arthurs Seat at 1.8 kilometres. As with a number of maps available, not all tracks and paths are shown. Use your judgement as required. It was interesting to note that my Navman, a GPS driven tool, took over 10 minutes to 'acquire' satellites. With a dense tree canopy, overcast skies and the undulating nature of the terrain do not rely solely on electronic devices. (Thanks to my son Rohan, who gave me this wonderful birthday present some years ago.)

Ruins on The Friends Track.

The walking path has some small boardwalks and a few steps as it winds its way towards Arthurs Seat. Some highlights on this track include an extensive glade of tree ferns, which had shown particularly good growth after the extensive rains of 2011. Maiden hair ferns were in abundance and as I was walking fairly quietly, I shouldn't have been surprised to see a wallaby bounding off into the bush. Further along, the track became a little overgrown with bracken fern and wire grass. Very intriguing are the remains of a stone ruin, pictured, which must surely have a story to tell. This stone ruin is almost 1 kilometre from the start of the T intersection with the OT Dam track. Perhaps in time Parks Victoria and the Friends of Arthurs Seat may be able to identify this former dwelling and the inhabitants from possibly the 1800's!

At around 1.1 kilometres you will intersect with a main access road to the quarry. You pass through walkers turnstiles and barriers, before crossing this road and continuing toward the Arthurs Seat Road. Return along the Arthurs Seat Road, utilizing the equestrian trail or return the way you came for a quieter experience.

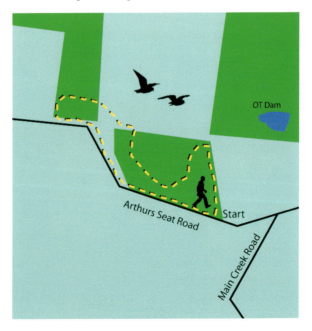

BALBIROOROO WETLANDS BALNARRING

This is a great location for a short and interesting walk to suit all ages. Plenty of variation with birds to hear and see, whether from bird hides or the track itself. Information boards give details of the flora and fauna in this area. Come and experience a peaceful part of the 'Westernport' precinct.

Start	End of Civic Court, Balnarring
Distance	Less than 2 kilometres
Time	20 minutes to 1+ hour
Grade	Flat, some boardwalks
Maps	Melways: Map 193 C6
When	Anytime
Note	Stroller friendly, partially sheltered

While there is limited parking in Civic Court, the only time this may be an issue is at the start and end of the school day. There is signage en route on the wetlands flora and fauna as well as a photo of the opening of the Redhill Railway in 1923.

Start your walk, passing the Balnarring Primary School and walking in a clockwise direction. The wide, gravel path makes for easy walking

There were many Black Swans in residence on my recent autumn visit. On the western side of the small lake is an excellent bird hide which looks out towards some nesting boxes. Three water hens were also in evidence as I walked my way quietly along the path. Part of the track

Balbirooroo Wetlands.

required a small amount of maintenance, so take care if you have the elderly or children in your group. Board walks are always interesting. Younger children find them particularly attractive as they cannot get lost or get too far off the beaten track.

Listen for the sounds of frogs and the many birds which inhabit the area.

While there are some alternative routes to take along the board walk, there is little chance of getting lost here. Balbirooroo Wetlands is a very picturesque location. Being suitable for younger families, this walk is high on interest and short on effort. The walk could be shortened to 20 minutes or lengthened to well over an hour with a picnic hamper ready to be consumed at one of the strategically placed picnic tables. There is a delightful spot under the eucalypt trees for such a picnic and the adjacent board walk will give smaller members of your family an excellent vantage point to gain glimpses of any wildlife in the area.

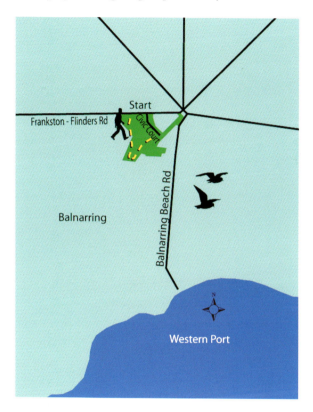

BALCOMBE ESTUARY NATURE PARK TRAIL

This very popular boardwalk is remarkable for its length, its sheltered canopy of trees and forest and its picturesque nature. Impossible to get lost, easy on the feet and with a café stop at the halfway point, who can resist the temptation?

Start	The Briars Park Information Centre, Mount Martha
Distance	7 kilometres return
Time	2+ hours return
Grade	Easy
Maps	Melways: Map 145 F12, Balcombe Estuary Reserve pamphlet
When	Anytime
Suggestion	Café lunch at Mt Martha Village

Be sure to visit the Information Centre prior to your walk. There is a wealth of exhibits here as well as brochures and other displays.

The track to Balcombe Estuary is well sign-posted and part of the boardwalk was in the process of being upgraded on my last visit. Without too many stops you will reach Mt Martha Beach within the hour. However there are many points-of-interest along the way.

With the recent summer rains the creek appeared to be in good condition with relatively clear water, bright green plant growth showing through with some of the water-based plants.

A newly constructed Boardwalk, which you may notice on your

drive into the park, leads to a new revegetation area and is also worth investigating. This is Harrap Creek, a Melbourne Water initiative. Around 500 metres of walking will have you passing below the Nepean Highway bridge. Continue past part of the former Balcombe Army Camp training area. My late uncle, Dr Adrian Hughes, vividly remembered his wartime stint at the Balcombe Army Camp, having gained exemption from his dental studies during the wartime. He particularly recalled sleeping on hay bales in the cold of winter and also walking into Frankston just to go to the 'pub' on Saturday night. (Information signage located near the barbecue facilities at the end of the Mirang Avenue, further describes the military occupation, 70 years ago, which involved four thousand troops.)

The track is probably around 80% boardwalk all away to the Esplanade at Mount Martha Village. The track is relatively well signposted to Port Phillip Bay despite a number of twists and turns. There are many side tracks which return you to residential streets abutting this reserve. If you inadvertently take the wrong turn it is a matter of only a few minutes before you are back on the right track. Try to keep as close as possible to the creek heading towards Port Phillip Bay which is approximately due West.

There are some strategically placed seats en route, some overlooking the estuary itself and those may be the perfect places to regroup or simply enjoy the tranquillity of a different part of the peninsula. When I am conducting a group walk I like to 're-group' every half hour, on the half hour. This way everyone in the group knows when they will meet up with the other walkers. While 30 minutes on this route may be too long between stops, the principle is a good one that assures slower walkers and those taking the time to read the signage en route that they will not be forgotten or left behind.

The area at the end of the walk, abutting Mirang Avenue, is in need of an injection of funds if only to keep grounds maintenance and grass cutting up to the mark. This boardwalk is a wonderful community asset. Replacement value today could well be in the millions of dollars

Balcombe Estuary Boardwalk.

and there would probably be enough work for one full time person to maintain this entire length of track. Runners and joggers, young families with strollers, families with young children on bicycles, walkers and retirees, and even young 'lovers' using one of the seats on a brilliant autumn afternoon: all use this track, reserve and boardwalk on a regular basis. Estimates are that 50 000 walking visits are made here every year! Perhaps assets such as these should not be left solely to the volunteer groups that abound on the peninsula, in this case Balcombe Estuary Rehabilitation Group.

At this point in your walk, having reached the beach, civilisation and the retail precinct, the choices are to have a picnic on the beach, a cafe stop in Mount Martha Village or simply to return after utilising the barbecue picnic area and the children's playground equipment, as required. This is a very interesting walk that should not be missed.

This walk was constructed between 1986 and 2001.

For further information on the Balcombe Estuary Rehabilitation Group visit: www.berg.org.au

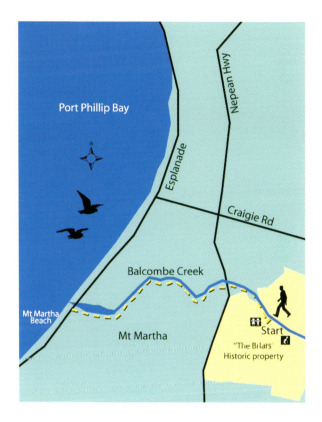

BALD HILL NATURE CONSERVATION RESERVE

6

Panoramic views towards Safety Beach and Mt Martha as well as a less well-known walking venue make this quiet location an ideal place to get away from it all and stretch your legs. This is a loop walk with a reasonably steep gradient on the return leg. This is a short walk with interesting flora to add to your enjoyment.

Start	Bowrings Road, Red Hill
Distance	3 kilometres
Time	Approximately 45 minutes
Grade	Medium, reasonably steep return track
Maps	Melways 161 B11
When	Anytime

There is very limited parking at the intersection of Bowrings Road and Browns Lane. The gated entry is only for management vehicles and walkers can follow the 4WD track in a basic loop to complete this scenic walk in well under 1 hour. Follow the very pleasant bush track, taking the left fork immediately inside the gate. There is a slight climb and you will pass impressive stands of eucalyptus trees in this quiet and peaceful setting. Great views towards Martha Point, Dromana and the lush agricultural hinterland which has greatly

benefited from a wet summer season are all on show here. Obviously, choose a fine day with clear skies for optimum views. Take binoculars if they are available. The Dandenong's, Port Phillip Bay, Mount Eliza,

Bald Hill Nature Conservation Reserve.

the Melbourne CBD skyline and the You Yangs are all visible from various vantage points along this walk.

When you arrive at a fork in the 4WD track take the right hand route which passes an old survey marker, a Trig. Point. The track descends fairly steeply to a boundary fence and continues in a westerly direction until the climb commences. Part of the ascent is possibly around 30 degrees in gradient and walkers should exercise care when negotiating this section of the route. Take care on the loose gravel as this can be slippery. Some years ago a young woman in our walking group suffered a hairline fracture after falling in similar terrain.

Walking poles would be a distinct advantage, particularly if you need additional support. I have only seen one other person when I have undertaken this hike. It's a special place, seldom frequented by the throngs of holiday makers that head for the beaches, golf courses and wineries which make the Peninsula famous. Enjoy.

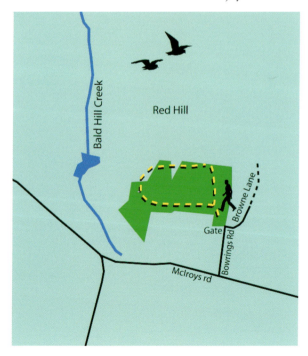

BALDRY CROSSING CIRCUIT

Take a walk in Greens Bush. Sheltered on windy days and with protection from summer sun, this idyllic location boasts good quality walking tracks, fern gullies, impressive eucalypt forests combined with several creek crossings over well maintained bridges. Come and enjoy a very popular part of the Peninsula.

Start	Baldry Crossing, Baldrys Road, Main Ridge
Distance	3.6 kilometres return
Time	Around 1 hour
Grade	Medium, steps and pathway
Maps	Melways: Map 254 G6
When	Anytime except Total Fire Ban and Code Red Days

The walk starts at the carpark adjacent to Main Creek and Splitters Creek. The carpark has one picnic table and an old barbeque. On weekends and holiday periods this can be a very popular walk. But mid-week and mid-winter you may be lucky to see a single soul!

Cross the road, and follow the track alongside the creek. Signage indicates 3.4 km for the longer circuit. Within 100 metres there is an information shelter which includes a large scale map, the contribution of the Greens family to this fabulous area and information on cinnamon fungus. The first part of the walk along the creek is absolutely delightful. Good winter rain had given Main Creek a solid flow of water with a distinct babbling sound as it made its way towards Bushrangers

Baldry Crossing Circuit.

Bay. A walk during the winter months allows the walker to see the profusion of mosses as well as the vivid green colour of the new fronds of bracken fern. The first part of this track is well maintained with the bonus of a carpet of leaves. The track is initially flat and is certainly easy walking.

Before long there is an ascent up some steps. This higher ground gives you great views of Main Creek, tree ferns abutting the creek and the cleared farming land to the south. This immediate area is quite reminiscent of the Otways, particularly around the Lorne area and Phantom Falls. As the track gradually started to ascend it became muddy and slippery in places requiring a little extra care. Approaching an intersection which indicates Baldry Crossing is 2.8 kilometres, take the left hand track. You will approach a boardwalk with chicken wire over the decking, which is certainly useful during damp winter days.

Passing the boardwalk, the track becomes carpeted with leaves again. Bracken fern was in abundance here and this particular part of the walk looked like a good place to encounter kangaroos, being fairly open forest.

The track now becomes decidedly wider, having been recently mown. Your next intersection is the Two Bays Walking Track. Baldry Crossing is now 2.6 kilometres away. Another boardwalk will speed you on your way. While a gale warning was forecast for adjacent Victorian waters when I last did this walk the forest was amply protected from the strong south westerly winds. The forest around you certainly has an array of vegetation from eucalyptus and acacias, banksia trees, sedges, sword grass, wire grass and tea tree, just to name a few. As you approach the gully tree ferns become obvious as well as a few bulrushes. A few isolated paper barks also make their presence felt. While the forest was protected from the prevailing winds there was obvious damage to one of the forest giants which had been torn apart by some seriously strong winds.

Another walking track intersection which is part of the Two Bays Walking Track and the Baldry Crossing circuit indicates that is only 1.8 km back to the start of the walk. Pass another small creek which has water flowing in the winter. While the water was rust coloured it was sufficiently clear to see the bottom of the creek bed. This surely augurs well for the health of these waterways and the flora and fauna which are dependent on this waterway. The more elevated parts of this walking track were very dry in the winter and made for easy walking. As you get nearer to the Baldry Crossing carpark you sight farming paddocks on the other side of Main Creek which you passed at the beginning of your walk. Take the left hand track, using the map at this particular intersection, to return you to the start of your walk. On this high ridge you will notice numerous grass trees which were showing the benefits of the moist summer and good winter rain. The track now becomes wider, being used by management vehicles from time to time. I can now hear vehicular traffic. The equestrian trail sign is a few metres away and you are extremely close to the end of your walk. The exit point is about 50 metres north of the entry point to this walk.

Note: There is a shorter circuit of 1.6 kilometres which is well signposted if you are pressed for time or require a slightly easier walk. This area has a resident kangaroo population. Road signage indicates this fact. Take particular care at dawn and dusk when you are driving. Over the years I have seen a number of dead kangaroos on the side of the roads throughout this area.

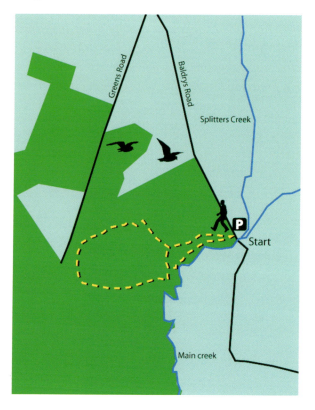

BALNARRING BEACH TO MERRICKS CREEK

Get away from the crowds and explore a less frequented part of the coastline of Westernport Bay. Merricks Creek, with its distinctive suspension bridge, is a feature of this walk. A relaxing trek on a protected beach with some walking through wetlands adjacent to Coolart Homestead.

Start	Carpark and Rotunda, Balnarring Beach Road
Distance	4 kilometres return
Time	90 minutes for reasonably paced walkers
Grade	Easy with sandy beaches
Maps	Melways Map 193 D10, Parknotes, Parks Victoria: Coolart Wetlands and Homestead
When	Anytime
Option	Extend this walk by heading for Somers Beach, add 4 kilometres return and an extra hour

The Balnarring Beach rotunda is your stepping off point for the start of this hike. The gravel car park adjacent to the beach rotunda has ample parking at most times of the year. Signage at the entrance to the beach recognizes the Boonerwong people, the traditional owners of the area.

This walk starts on a great ocean beach. Before heading off to the left and Somers there is an interesting headland around 200 metres distant, to your right. This feature is so close that it 'begs' your interest and your explorative streak. This is well worth the effort as the area is a

Balnarring Beach.

bird sanctuary and recent plantings have added to the appeal of this location. Views of Point Leo and West Head at Flinders can be gained by walking around the small headland. Notice the rocks on the headland which have been placed there to prevent erosion.

Heading back to the main part of your walk, 'strike out' for Somers beach. The firm sand is an excellent base for walking and a good, steady pace should come easily on all but the highest of tides where you may have to walk on softer sand closer to the foreshore reserve. As you approach Westernport Yacht Club there is a small jetty. The club will be buzzing with activity over the warmer months but for most of the year this a very peaceful beach particularly in the off-season. Binoculars could be handy to look at ships in the bay as well as distant views of Phillip Island. Continue walking along the beach, keeping an eye out for any interesting flotsam and jetsam washed up amongst the seaweed.

More particularly, sea dragons are known to inhabit the area and more rarely paper nautilus shells can wash up on this coastline.

About one kilometre from the start of your walk is a track which leads to a bridge. This will take you into the back waters of Merricks Creek and the Coolart Wetlands precinct. Another kilometre of walking allows you to experience this different part of the foreshore reserve. Forested, with birds and more sheltered from the elements, the wetlands tracks, walking loops 2, 3 and 4, offer a contrast to the wide open spaces of the coastline and beach walk. Return to the beach and then decide if you wish to walk to the mouth of Merricks Creek or return to the rotunda at Balnarring Beach.

Note: Very high tides, as experienced at Easter, and strong east to south-east winds can make this walk arduous.

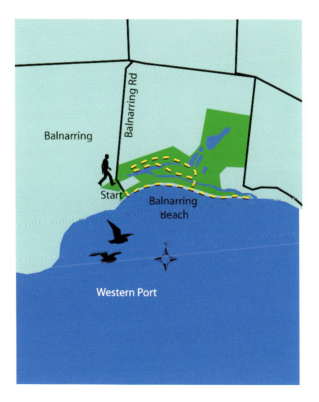

BLOW HOLE TRACK FLINDERS

Rugged and wild, the Blow Hole can be a spectacular sight with raw ocean swell breaking over the basalt cliffs. See nature in its fundamental form, untamed and powerful, a statement in grand design.

Start	Blow Hole Track, Flinders
Distance	750 metres
Time	30 minutes
Grade	Medium with steps
Maps	Melways map 261 D11
When	Any time
Warning	Exercise extreme caution in this area. Be very careful with high tides and large swell.

After taking in the views from the observation area, walk down towards the coastline. The track and stairway are well maintained and within a few minutes you will arrive at the shoreline. This is not your average 'beach'. With black volcanic rock, the basalt forms an uncharacteristic beach of black sand and water-worn volcanic rocks. Continue to your left, walking along the 'beach' and out onto a rock platform if conditions are safe. If you are at all unsure of the sea conditions, err on the side of caution and keep well back from the waters edge. Large waves can surge up high onto the rock platform with little warning.

Slowly return to the carpark, taking the time to observe this majestic location. Once back at the observation area, follow the walking track

Blow Hole at Flinders.

to the west, towards Cape Schanck. This track continues for about 250 metres and terminates at a small 'beach' on the shoreline. Again, exercise extreme caution if you are unfamiliar with the ocean and surf. Pay particular attention to children and ensure they do not venture to close to the water. Look out for interesting pieces of debris left on the high tide line. The author has found many items washed up along the Bass Strait coastline including fishing gear, a diving knife, a fishing buoy with Argentine markings and even interesting varieties of 'dried' fish. You may be fortunate to see shorebirds such as gannets and mutton birds along this part of the coast. As well, the constant procession of container ships and freighters may also be a part of your viewing from this location.

Simply retrace your steps to return to the start of the walk.

Just as I had completed re-writing this walk there had been another fatality at this location. A surf fisherman was washed into the ocean. Please take extreme care.

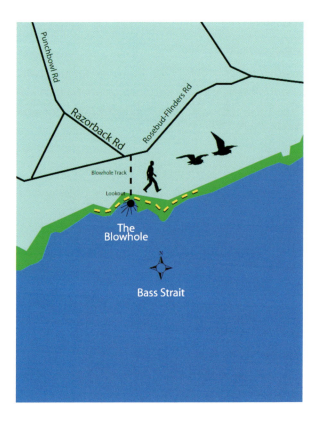

BRIARS WETLANDS AND WOODLANDS RESERVE

The Briars Park has much to offer nature lovers, walkers and especially bird observers. This 'not to be missed' venue has an information centre which will keep children enthused for some time and a comfortable bird hide with seats will appeal to all walkers of all ages.

Start	Entry via Nepean Highway, Mt Martha.
Distance	Under 4 kilometres return. Only 400 metres to Chechingurk Bird Hide
Time	Allow at least 2 Hours
Effort	Easy, undulating
Maps	Melways 145 F12
When	Any time of the year except Christmas Day and Good Friday
Contact	Visitor Centre 5974 3686 or the.briars@mornpen.vic.gov.au Open 9 am to 5 pm except Christmas Day and Good Friday

A detailed map is freely available at the Information Centre which outlines the three walks, listed below, and gives excellent coverage of the many aspects of this location. Also at the centre are documentaries on the park and the historic Briars Homestead.

The Briars Wetlands and Woodlands Reserve is one of the few parts of the Mornington Peninsula that has stands of some of the original vegetation particularly Manna and Swamp Eucalypts.

Briars Wetlands and Woodlands Wildlife Reserve.

Start your walk by heading out on the 'Wetland Walk' to the Chechingurk (Bird) Hide, under half a kilometre from the Information Centre. Small information boards detail some of the various species of vegetation which are found along this walk. There are numerous seats along the tracks and this makes for a good stopping point if you have faster walkers.

The tracks within the park are all very well sign-posted. There are many bird charts within the bird hide as well as some exhibits. The carpeted hide is one of the most comfortable bird hides on the peninsula so please take the time to enjoy this great facility.

Retrace your path until the next walking track T intersection. This is the clearly marked link-track, (Tichin-Gorourke Link). Take the right hand track and head out towards the Ker-Bur-Rer walk. This is the longest of three walks available within this reserve. The next track intersection is a viewing platform which gives panoramic views of the wetlands and the surrounding countryside. Now that the long drought is well and truly behind us, this area has come alive again as a major rookery and nesting area for some of the 214 species of birds that inhabit the Mornington Peninsula.

From the viewing platform the track now becomes a bushwalkers track, narrower and more undulating but with the added feature of well-placed seats every few hundred metres.

After leaving the viewpoint there is an extensive stand of bulrushes along Balcombe Creek. A tall stand of Paperbarks is also very evident here. At the north-eastern most point a farmhouse can be seen. Now the track changes direction and ascends to the top of a small hill. Ginna's Dam is on the top of this hill and the vegetation becomes more open and scrubby. You will cross another emergency vehicle access track and pass Spring Paddock Dam before descending towards the Information Centre, the security gate exit and your vehicle.

There is so much to do and see within 'The Briars Park' that I recommend you allow a few hours to visit the nursery and perhaps the restaurant or have a barbeque at the conclusion of your walk. Why not allow up to half a day to take in this tranquillity and features the Briars has to offer.

A couple of years ago I was privileged to accompany members from Bird Observation and Conservation Australia on a tour of the park. It was a fantastic experience, having experts in the field to point out the different species of birds as well as offering tips on observation. They recommend binoculars of 8 by 40 magnification. Early morning or late evening are preferred viewing times and if possible have the sun behind you. Also be prepared to stay in one position and avoid heavy rain and hot and windy conditions too.

The Briars has brown goshawks, ducks, parrots, crimson rosellas, the superb fairy wren, the new holland honey eater and many more.

See boca.org.au

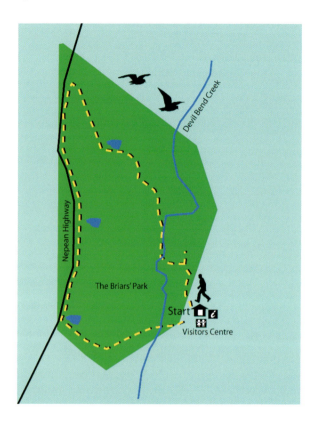

BUCKLEY NATURE CONCERVATION RESERVE

11

A newer addition to the array of reserves on offer throughout the Mornington Peninsula, Buckley Reserve is a loop walk which takes you through a variety of vegetation. Native orchids are on show during the warmer months of the year.

Start	Carpark, corner Myers and Balnarring Roads, Balnarring
Distance	2 kilometres circuit
Time	20 to 30 minutes for a group of walkers
Grade	Easy walking, possible creek crossing
Maps	Melways map 162 H7
When	Anytime

The starting point is at the corner of Myers and Balnarring Roads where there is ample parking. Walk in a south easterly direction on the wide four-wheel-drive management track. Traffic noise from the road is somewhat distracting, but it is only intermittent and the sounds of numerous species of birds become more apparent as you settle into a leisurely pace. Shortly you are at the southern entrance to the reserve, about 600 metres from the start of your walk.

Take the left hand track which heads in a northerly then north easterly direction. This part of the walk is noticeably quieter, there is a vineyard to your right. The different types of observable vegetation here may readily lend itself to a numbered nature trail. Perhaps this could be developed in the future. This is a peaceful and easy walk well within the capabilities of all walkers.

Buckley Nature Reserve.

As with any bushwalk where there is a water source, take care with snakes in the warmer months of the year. Remember snakes can still be active in spring and autumn. Approaching the north eastern entry point to the reserve, you now turn left and walk parallel to Myers Road. This is a great autumn mid-week walk, peaceful with numerous birds chortling and the sun filtering through the trees.

As you approach the end of this walk there is a temptation to take the left hand four-wheel-drive track. Continue straight ahead on the narrower and less defined walking track which eventually meets a small boardwalk which traverses Merrick's Creek. There is a good stand of paper bark trees here and some fish bone ferns were also in evidence. Well done, you've completed another walk!

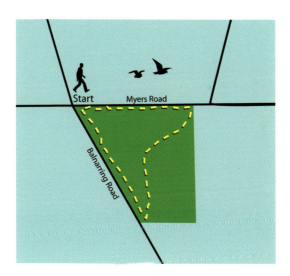

CAPE SCHANCK LIGHTHOUSE AND BUSHRANGERS BAY

A standout location with spectacular, elevated views, place Cape Schanck on your 'must visit' list. Be it storm and strong winds or a perfect summers day, come and see one of the 'high points' of the peninsula. Lighthouses have their own attractions and the lightstation and surrounding infrastructure is very worthy of your time.

Start	Carpark , Cape Schanck
Grade	Medium
Distance	7 kilometres including Bushrangers Bay and Pulpit Rock
Time	Allow 2 to 3 hours
Map	Melways map 257, 258, Parknotes: Discovering Cape Schanck
When	Almost anytime

If you haven't visited Cape Schanck for a few years you will be in for a pleasant surprise. Not only have admission fees been abolished but the car park and facilities have had a serious upgrade. For first time visitors to the area, you are in for a treat.

There are three main walks to cover at the 'Schanck'. Bushrangers Bay, Pulpit Rock and the Cape and Lighthouse surrounds.

Bushrangers Bay is named after bushrangers who made landfall here in 1853. The walking track is well signposted and the distance is shown

Pulpit Rock by Charlotte George.

as 2.6 kilometres. First stop is a lookout only 150 metres away with commanding views to Bushrangers Bay and the coastline beyond to Phillip Island.

The Bushrangers Bay coastal nature walk comprises twelve locations on the track that cover the flora and fauna, geology and social history of this unique area. Discovering Cape Schanck, Bushrangers Bay Coastal Nature Walk: Guide and Information Booklet is available from the kiosk at the Cape Schanck lighthouse and is highly recommended. This booklet details the features of this highly acclaimed walk.

The track itself is well formed, gravelled in parts and earthen elsewhere with rubberised matting in particular sections. There are steps and stairs en route.

The first stop has a well positioned seat which overlooks Cape Schanck and Pulpit Rock, much of this geology is the result of a lava flow which occurred about 60 million years ago. The second viewing point will have you appreciating the sea sculpturing effect of the salt laden wind, which prunes the tightly clinging cliff face vegetation.

On a late autumn day with rain clouds threatening to blow in from Bass Strait, and the commercial fishing season finished, there wasn't even a single containership to be seen anywhere. With over 3000 movements of large ships entering port Phillip Bay yearly you can expect to see at least one or two ships about the Cape Schanck area.

The fit and enthusiastic walkers may well manage up to 6 kilometres per hour on the flat sections of this track. That's what my Navman was indicating on a recent trip to the area. The track is initially undulating with many flat sections but there are some small rise and falls.

Interestingly, I sighted another walker heading back to the Cape Schanck carpark. Sporting a good pair of binoculars but nothing in the way of back pack, coat, water or any of the other requisites and sensible walkers should carry, I was amazed but not surprised. With 3 walkers lost in Victoria in recent months the message does not always get out to those who need to hear it most. Be prepared. Over-cater for your hike. Take more than you need: Even the inclusion of matches, a seemingly nonsensical item for walking, may prove a life-saver if you are lost in cold conditions or need to attract attention in a remote area.

Elephant Rock at Bushrangers Bay.

During wetter months parts of this track can be muddy, however these obstacles are easily negotiated. The walk continues with more glimpses of Bass Strait and also views of the lush pastures to your left. Farming has been carried on here for well over 150 years. As you continue walking you will enter a virtual tunnel of tea tree, this feature offers protection from wind, sun and light. Surprisingly, erosion is also an issue along this part of the track, even though we are well over 100 metres above sea level, the wind still makes its presence felt.

Approach Burrabong Creek there are a number of steps to negotiate before the stairway and small wooden bridge. Very shortly you will be ascending and then regaining a relatively flat track as you head for the Bushrangers Bay and the Boneo Road track intersection. At the track junction it is 2.4 kilometres to Boneo Road. Better still the beach is only 160 metres: hooray!

My walking time was 40 minutes one way with some short stops. This was a power walk with few stops. Certainly add more time if you intend stopping at each of the 12 observation places, if you have a number of people in your group and you are doing it as part of a relaxation exercise more than a physical workout.

Once on the beach at Bushrangers Bay make a careful assessment of the creek depth and tide conditions before crossing this creek. In summer on a low tide there may be no obstacle whatsoever. With winter rains, an incoming tide and heavy swell this creek could become impassable and it could be quite dangerous to attempt a crossing. Please err on the side of caution. You are a long way from help here. Mobile phone (except satellite) and UHF radio coverage may not be available.

For the return trip, the 'climb' out of Bushrangers Bay is substantial and will take a reasonable effort. There is the 40 metre climb back to the track junction. Whether my age is getting the better of me, or the 30 kilometre bike ride that morning had sapped my energy, this was certainly a heart raising exercise. From the track junction it is a steady climb walking back to Burrabong Creek, then there are some steps again before the track levels out as it skirts the coast back to Cape Schanck. And I had just realised I had left my first aid kit in the car! After being very critical of the previous walker who was carrying only his binoculars… don't cast the first stone. I must also investigate the psychology behind the fact that the return hikes always seemed longer than when you are heading out to your destination. My return journey was done in half an hour almost non-stop, and up to almost 7 kilometres per hour on the flat sections of the track. Time for a rest.

Cape Schanck Lightstation. More a sightseeing tour than a walk, never-the-less, visitors to the area must include this on their itinerary. Allow up to an hour for a tour of the actual lighthouse and associated grounds and buildings.

A small entry fee applies. Distance approximately 500 metres.

Cape Schanck and Pulpit Rock. This is a serious descent from the top of the stairs to the bottom on the stairway and boardwalk adjacent to Pulpit Rock. The first part of the walk is on a gravel track. Those walkers who are less enthusiastic may prefer to terminate their walk at the top of the stairway, where great views of the 'Schanck' are possible. Once at the bottom of the stairway walkers may wish to venture out to the rocky beach and rock platform. Please exercise extreme caution here. People have been washed off the rocks here. The water is over 60 metres deep close to shore and large ocean swell can break over these rocks at any time. If you have children in your walking group, please play it safe and take no risks.

For walkers with further aspirations, note the last gravel road on your left before the entry into Cape Schanck carpark. Signage here indicates Gunnamatta at 7.6 kilometres. There is a well-maintained walking track which passes the Fingal Picnic Area. There are further spectacular views along this part of the track from a number of lookouts. See walk number 20 for details of part of the walk to Gunnamatta.

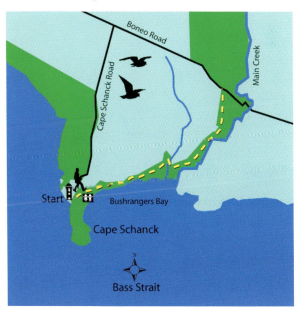

CHINAMANS CREEK, WEST ROSEBUD TO RYE

A typical bayside walk, easy on the eye and easy on the feet, with cafes en route for a lunch break or thirst quencher. Colourful boatsheds, stacks of beach-goers and campers over the summer months and quiet and almost desolate during the mid-week, mid-winter time frame. Take your choice.

Start	Chinamans Creek, West Rosebud
Distance	Up to 10 kilometres return
Time	2+ hours return
Grade	Easy and very flat
Maps	Melways 169 J2
When	Anytime
Option	Walking track in one direction and return by the beach

Start your walk at the Capel Sounds Camping Ground, West Rosebud. This area has seen massive improvement in recent years. Camping facilities here are now amongst some of the best on the peninsula. The beach has been nominated for cleanest beach in Australia. This beach was the winner of the Keep Australia Beautiful Victoria, Clean Beach Challenge 2008. Extensive re-vegetation has occurred along this section of Port Philip Bay thanks in part to the Friends of Chinamans Creek and Rosebud Secondary College to name but two.

At quieter times of the year, please take the time to walk to the mouth of Chinamans Creek. (Even though the Melways describe this as a

Chinamans Creek.

drain!) The area is now very attractive thanks to dedicated volunteers who have spent hundreds of hours to re-vegetate this location. As well, large numbers of shorebirds frequent this area, particularly at the mouth of the creek. Black swans, cormorants, white-faced herons, pacific and silver gulls, terns and the occasional pelican all make their presence felt here from time to time.

The decision to be made at the commencement of your walk is either to walk along the beach or take the bike and pedestrian path that winds its way through the foreshore. Observe the prevailing winds, tide level and weather forecast to make a call on the best option. With strong westerly and north-westerly wind it may be prudent to walk on the path to Rye and return along the beach with a tail-wind advantage.

There's no chance of getting lost here. Everything is very straight forward. Mobile reception is guaranteed and there are usually any number of helpful walkers, joggers and cyclists to offer help or 'directions' if required.

When walking along the path take care when crossing any vehicular tracks or when near the boat ramp at Tootgarook. Some cyclists ride a little too fast so watch out for blind bends in the shared pathway where visibility is restricted. Apart from this small hazard your walk will be enjoyable and interesting.

Approaching Rye township there is a popular venue for kite and wind surfers. On any windy day it will be hard to miss the action. Kite surfing, in particular, has really taken off recently. It's a spectacular sport and

Rye Jetty and Arthurs Seat.

this will keep all walkers entertained for some time as you see some amazing skills and airborne acrobatics demonstrated.

The Rye Yacht Club is the next point of interest as you approach the impressive Rye pier and the Rye boat ramp. Again, over the warmer months, these areas will be hives of activity and it may well be worth while to have a short break and take in the sights before retracing your steps to the start of your walk. Bus 788 could always be used to return you to your vehicle.

Note: There are ample facilities on the Rye foreshore including playground equipment for the younger people in your group. Picnic tables, barbecues, amenities blocks, a wide choice of eateries and a hotel as well as a number of choices for ice creams, if required.

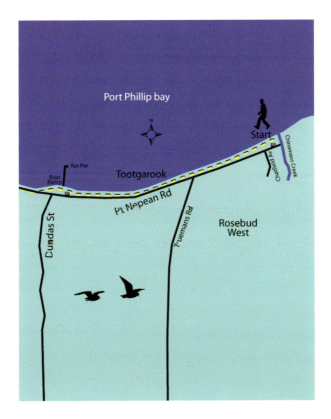

COOLART WETLANDS AND HOMESTEAD

Experience a stately mansion from a by-gone era with its impressive and expansive gardens. The wetlands adjacent to this historic property as well as the foreshore precinct all add a special atmosphere to this unique part of the peninsula. Walk on a suspension bridge and experience the quieter shores of Westernport Bay.

Start	Information Centre, Lord Somers Road, Somers
Distance	Up to 3 kilometres return
Time	Allow 2+ hours return
Grade	Medium, undulating
Maps	Melways map 193 H9, Parknotes: Coolart Wetlands and Homestead Visitor Guide
When	The park is open from 10.00am to 5.00pm every day except Christmas Day, Boxing Day and Good Friday.
Suggestion	Have lunch at the picnic facilities which include barbecues

Before commencing your walk be sure to investigate the Visitor Centre, which includes literature, static displays and a daily audio visual presentation at 1-30 pm.

Start walking, heading to Luxton Lagoon (Coolart Lagoon on your Melways) and the Minsmere (Bird) Hide. Keep bearing right and it is relatively easy, with good signage, to arrive at Minsmere Hide. I was

Merricks Creek and Suspension Bridge.

disappointed on my last visit to the hide as there were very few ibis in residence on the small island sanctuary. On a previous visit the island was covered with birds. July to November is the nesting season. While there were not as many birds present, the lagoon was overflowing from recent good rainfall. With 15 millimetres of overnight rain the pastures looked particularly green and lush. Please take care with young children in your group as areas such as this could harbour snakes in the drier months of the year.

Returning from the Minsmere Hide pick up the first gravel path and grass track on your right which eventually heads towards the beach. This track skirts an adjacent farming property before heading right and to the east. Before long you will arrive at a track intersection where three post-and rail 'fences' have been erected. Take the signed track to the beach. This is your next way-point or intermediate destination.

The paths and tracks around the wetland areas are a great walk for young kids as there is plenty of 'hide and seek' with twists and turns in the tracks. There are any number of water hens to be seen scurrying about and taking flight as they try to get some distance between themselves and human intruders.

As you approach the beach you may hear the surf as you now walk over a wooden bridge to cross Merricks Creek. On your left you can see the white painted suspension bridge, further downstream, which you will use on your return after a short beach walk.

Entering the beach on a winters day I instantly found the wind to be cold and strong after the relative shelter of the forest walk. With these noticeably cooler conditions it was time to cover up with a light parka from the day pack to break the impact of the southerly winds. The forecast for the day had indicated snowfalls down to 900 metres. When you arrive on the beach turn right and head for the suspension bridge, about 500 metres to the east.

With this cold air mass there was excellent visibility and I was able to count the individual houses across the bay at Ventnor on Phillip Island. As you walk along the beach, Sandy Point will come into view. Look for a wide track to your left and the suspension bridge should now come into view. Negotiate this impressive wooden bridge over Merricks Creek which is called the Somers School Camp bridge.

Take the track on the left, passing the cyclone fence, walk over a stile and onto a small walking track. This track had not been well used and was a little overgrown at the time of writing. Shortly this track meets a gravel road. Bear right and this will take you all the way to the Coolart Homestead and wetlands precinct. Notice the tree guards to protect the eucalypts from possum and koala damage. The track here is relatively high in elevation with occasional glimpses towards Western Port Bay. You will pass the point where, earlier, you headed towards the beach. Notice the three post and rail structures again and take the right hand track back towards the homestead.

Your 'Coolart Wetlands and Homestead' map, courtesy of Parks Victoria, is very useful and is highly recommended, whether downloading the PDF from the Parks Victoria website or from the Visitor Centre.

Having arrived at the homestead take the time to step into the stately mansion and enjoy the 'English' gardens of Coolart. I noticed a quince tree 'in season' bearing its fruit. The gardens, with many specimen trees, is very well maintained and is in stark contrast to the coastal vegetation which has been your companion for the larger part of your walk. Walk through the gardens to return to your vehicle.

Note: Many of the tracks at Coolart are suitable for baby strollers.

DEVILBEND RESERVOIR

15

A peaceful location that readily lends itself to a family picnic or lunchtime break. While the walk is very short there are great views of this impressive water storage. The Devilbend Reservoir is a scenic locale, often overlooked by visitors to the area but its charm will be heightened when greater public access is granted in the coming years.

Start	Graydens Road, Mooroduc South
Distance	Up to 1 kilometre
Time	Under 1 hour with a picnic stop
Grade	Easy
Maps	Melways Map 152 J3
When	All Year

Access to the picnic area is via Graydens Road. This is a gravel road so travel slowly and take note of the travel advisory signs. The lawns here at this small picnic area were again very green and well maintained on my most recent walk. The expanse of mown lawns may lend themselves to a ball game with any younger children in your group. While there are minimal facilities, tables being a bonus, the tranquillity of the area more than compensates for these slight deprivations. While most of the Mornington Peninsula may hum with visitors during the busier holiday periods, it is likely that Devilbend Reservoir will be very peaceful and free from crowds. There is ample room for vehicle parking.

Walking around the fence line gives views towards the Devilbend Dam wall and views towards Main Ridge. The actual dam wall and associated

Devilbend Reservoir.

Spring Wildflowers at Devilbend Reservoir.

infrastructure is quite impressive. An added plus on my autumn visit were rosellas. They were busily feasting on native blooms in the vicinity. I'm sure families with children will find there is ample to do here.

Take care if you walk across the dam wall roadway from the picnic area to the overflow. There is no pedestrian walkway or path, however traffic is usually very light at his location. This infrastructure was officially opened in 1965 by the then Premier of Victoria, Henry Bolte, of Bolte Bridge fame, City Link, Melbourne.

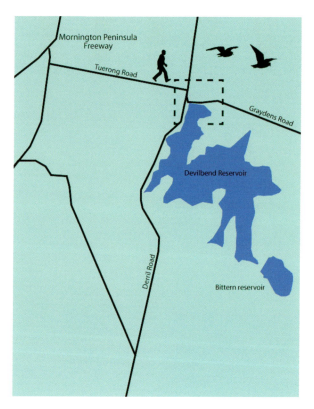

DROMANA TO ARTHURS SEAT

16

Come and experience the exhilaration of having walked to the top of the highest 'mountain' on the Mornington Peninsula. Take in the stunning views of the Port Philip Bay coastline and Bass Strait. This walk is not as difficult as it looks. On a clear day even the Otways will be visible. This is a photographers delight as well as a walkers challenge. The walk is part of the Two Bays Walking Track.

Start	Bunurong Track and Latrobe Parade, Dromana
Distance	4 kilometres return
Time	2+ hours
Grade	Medium. Please assess your fitness before undertaking this walk
Maps	Melways map 159 D8 or D10 www.visitmorningtonpeninsula.org/pdf/05_0289.pdf
When	Anytime, except Code Red days. Fine, clear forecast, wind below 10 knots.

For a shorter but never the-less challenging walk start at the Bunurong Track, where there is a small area for car parking. Walk through the gate on the mountain side of the Bunurong Track, displaying a sign 'Management Vehicles Only'. The walking track is well signposted, and in good condition and formed of gravel and stone in places. The track winds its way towards Seawinds at Arthurs Seat. As you can see from the detailed PDF map: Two Bays Walking Track', there are a number of side tracks that can take you to a number of destinations, be it the

Arthurs Seat Lookout.

Seawinds Gardens and the associated carpark and picnic facilities or the carpark and lookout on Arthurs Seat Road, adjacent to the restaurant. It can take around thirty minutes to arrive at the summit at Seawinds but with stops and rest breaks, depending on the age and capabilities of your walking group, this time will be longer. 'Slow and steady' is the way when walking uphill. Pace yourself so that you and the rest of your group are comfortably paced. You should be able to easily hold a conversation while walking.

Arthurs Seat looks massive when viewed from a distance. In fact it may look daunting at first. Don't be put off by what seems to be the enormity of the task. It is very 'do-able' and surprisingly easy for those who engage in regular walking or exercise program.

From the summit there are views of the McCrae Lighthouse, Rosebud

Safety Beach and Mt Martha.

Jetty and the greater part of Port Phillip Bay. On a clear day the views are astounding. Views from the summit adjacent to the restaurant also take in the Melbourne skyline on a clear day, parts of the Dandenongs, Westernport Bay and the You Yangs. I suggest you take binoculars.

For a longer walk and to complete part the Two Bays Walking Track, start from Dromana Beach, adjacent to the boat ramp at Anthonys Nose, Dromana and add nearly 2.7 kilometres. Walking commences opposite the Boat Ramp, just on the Melbourne side of Anthonys Nose. (Melways Map 159, C8). A forested walking track leads you to Latrobe Parade. There are some great views of the Dromana boathouses and beach from this short, steep track. Having arrived at Latrobe Parade, walk along the side of the road and over the Mornington Peninsula Freeway bridge before entering the Arthurs Seat forest adjacent to the Bunerong Track.

Note: I do not advise walking down Arthurs Seat Road for the return. There are blind hairpin bends, no footpath and virtually no room for pedestrians.

Wind chill factor: Also remember that it can be at least 3 degrees cooler at the summit of Arthurs Seat due to its elevation of over 300 metres. If there is a wind blowing the wind chill factor can be considerable. At 10C degrees with a wind speed of around 45 kph the wind chill factor will be around 0C degrees.

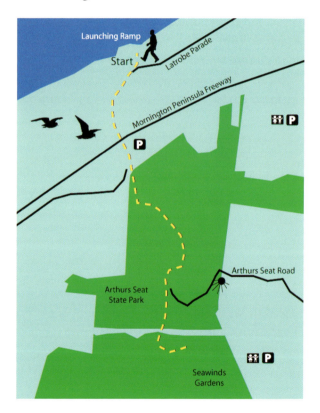

DROMANA, McCRAE LIGHTHOUSE AND ROSEBUD

Easy walking at any time of the year. Plenty to see and do. Boat sheds and coastal vegetation, the activity of the local yacht club and a boat ramp as well as throngs of campers over the summer season all add up for a walk which can be a special experience. The iconic McCrae Lighthouse and the narrow roadway where the bay meets Arthurs Seat are also part of the experience.

Start	Dromana Visitor information Centre, Corner Permien St and Point Nepean road, Dromana
Distance	9 kilometres return
Time	2 to 3 hours
Grade	Easy and flat
Maps	Melways map 159 F7
When	Anytime

Commence your walk opposite the Dromana Visitor Information Centre. The Visitor Centre is well worth a visit with up to the minute publications and accommodation guides as well as a comprehensive list of the many attractions and features on the Mornington Peninsula.

Head to the beach or walk along the more sheltered and flatter foreshore camping area if the tide is high or there is a strong headwind. As this is a return walk it is worth while considering walking along the beach one way and the other direction can be the 'inland' experience. The inland or foreshore track is part of the Bay Trail and it is well signposted.

McCrae Lighthouse.

As you head for Anthonys Nose ensure it is safe to walk along the waters edge. High tides and strong winds will see the waves breaking over the sea wall so take appropriate care.

Passing the sea wall, walk along the beach towards Rosebud, passing an assortment of colourful boatsheds. Over the warmer months the beach is a scene of activity with all types of water sports underway.

Along the McCrae and Dromana foreshores you see a huge array of camping equipment and caravans, pop-tops and tents during the camping season. This is an experience in itself, especially if you are considering purchasing camping gear in the near future.

The McCrae lighthouse is easy to spot and you may prefer to investigate this site on your return walk through the foreshore.

The McCrae lighthouse, built over 130 years ago, is essentially identical to the lighthouse at Currie, on King Island, Tasmania. My book "**Walks of King Island**," BAS Publishing, 2009, details an exploratory trek around the town, including the Currie lighthouse and museum. Unlike the McCrae Lighthouse, the King Island lighthouse has guided tours to the top of the lighthouse. Wouldn't it be great to be able to climb this lighthouse for a view too?

As you approach Rosebud Jetty, impossible to miss, you are nearing the halfway point of your walk. There are a number of cafes and eateries at Rosebud, McCrae and Dromana, so depending on the time of day you may like to consider a coffee or meal break or simply enjoy a pre-prepared picnic lunch on the foreshore where an adventure playground may entertain any smaller members of your group.

The return walk picks up the Two Bays Trail, readily signposted from the jetty. There is a boardwalk from the jetty which winds through foreshore vegetation before terminating at the foreshore and the beach. Continue through the foreshore, between the beach and Point Nepean Road. There are strategically placed amenities blocks along the way however some are available only for campers. As you near Anthonys

Nose again the foreshore narrows to only a few metres in width. Pick up the gravel buffer area behind the sea wall before passing the boat ramp and walking into the next camping area. About 750 metres east of Anthonys Nose pick up the Bay Trail walking track which will take you back to your vehicle.

This walk will suit families with strollers, the elderly and even young children with small bicycles. This track is also popular with joggers and power walkers. You will feel part of the crowd in this precinct. It is impossible to get lost here as you are always close to Point Nepean Road.

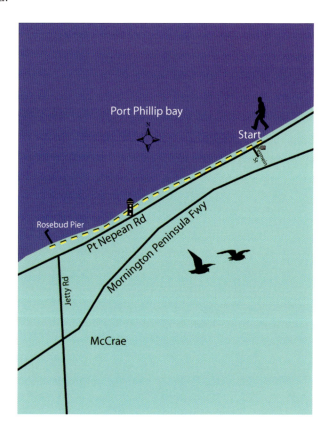

EATONS CUTTING CIRCUIT

18

Great views of Safety Beach, The Marina and the Dandenongs and beyond, as well as the rich agricultural area nearby are all possible on a clear day. This quieter part of the peninsula is easily walked and is a very rewarding loop circuit. Take your camera and binoculars too.

Start	Eatons Cutting Road, Red Hill
Distance	Around 1 kilometre
Time	45 minutes return
Grade	Easy Medium
Maps	Melways map 190 F1,
When	Avoid on Code Red days

The walk commences at the end of Eatons Cutting Road. I chose to walk in and anticlockwise direction, which is contrary to the blue direction arrows. The track is in good condition although parts of the eastern section of the track were a little over grown with bracken and long grass. Make your way towards a prominent, heavy duty, timber seat and vantage point which has views towards the Melbourne CBD, which was a little hazy on this particular day. Also look for Martha Point, Mount Martha and the expansive sweep of Port Phillip Bay.

After a stop at this great vantage point for a snack or drink, be sure to take a few photos as well. Continue on your way towards the commencement of this walk. Short on distance, big on view, come and visit Eatons Cutting Lookout, perhaps combining this short walk with a visit to one of the many local wineries.

Eatons Cutting Lookout.

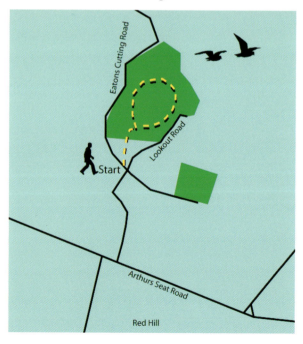

FINGAL BEACH AND SELWYN FAULT

Experience the rugged, exposed and untamed coastline that is Cape Schanck. Rock-hopping, small sandy coves, flotsam and jetsam from the Southern Ocean. This walk is for the adventurous. I started walking here in my teenage years and I'm still coming to one of my favourite places on the peninsula.

Start	Fingal Picnic Area, Cape Schanck
Distance	4+ kilometres
Time	Allow two hours
Grade	Easy along the beach, climbing the steps medium to hard
Maps	Melways Map 259 B9
When	Low tide only, under 0.3 metres. Low swell <1m
Suggestion	Walking pole or poles

Commence walking from the Fingal Picnic Area, Cape Schanck. Ensure all valuables are hidden from view in your vehicle. There is a clearly marked walking track down to Fingal Beach. At the sandy beach turn left towards Cape Schanck in a south westerly direction. The darker coloured basalt rocks were formed during volcanic activity some 60 million years ago.

Low tide walking allows for a faster transit over the rock platforms but take care while traversing wet rocks and rocks covered with seaweed. Walkers may find the numerous rock pools an interesting diversion. As this is a national park, take care not to disturb marine creatures living

Fingal Beach and Selwyn Fault.

in this intertidal zone. The rst small headland will come into view and as you negotiate this feature it may be prudent to use a handgrip where necessary to aid your balance. Notice the rst rocky 'beach' which may have items of flotsam and jetsam. This rock-strewn coastline can have much human debris, left by the high tides. I always spend some time fossicking here amongst the debris for signs of man's intervention as well as items of marine and biological derivation. Some years ago the author found a buoy marked: "Industrie de Argentina" washed up on this remote shore.

Carefully continue your expedition, this time out onto the rock platform again for a smoother walk between the numerous rock pools or up and over a series of large boulders and into the next small rocky cove. After rounding this next headland a small bay comes into view with a distinctive shoreline of larger basaltic rocky boulders. Continue walking into this small bay, where Selwyn Fault meets the coast. Selwyn Fault is a major geographical feature that runs through much of the Peninsula. This geological fault line was thought to be the major cause of a tremor in the 1930's which resulted in a quake of 6.0 at Mornington.

Again, keep an eye to seaward here at all times for large waves. Incoming tides and strong winds can both combine to produce waves which surge high up onto the shoreline. Do not attempt to reach the Cape Schanck lighthouse along this coastline. There is one very deep gulch, which will most certainly impede your progress and large waves often crash onto the rocky shoreline without warning. It is possible to get trapped in both directions along this section of coast. If sea conditions change and the swell starts to increase with an incoming tide, it is most definitely time to turn around and 'head for home'. Cape Schanck has claimed a number of lives over the years, please take care.

This walk is one of my favourite locations on the peninsula because there is a real sense of remoteness. It is not readily accessible to walkers and the towering cliffs add a dimension of awe and power to the experience. As well, close powers of observation must be exercised to continually monitor the state of the sea for maximum safety. For any walkers wanting to undertake some serious exploratory coastal walks, which are beyond the scope of this book, I offer a description from a publication entitled: Hiking, the essential guide to equipment and techniques: "When exploring sections of coastline, protective headgear and a PFD are essential and a wetsuit is preferable in cold water".

FINGAL PICNIC AREA AND BEACH CIRCUIT

Spectacular coastal scenery, changing vegetation, sand dunes, wide sandy beaches, tall cliffs and forested paths all add to the interest on this remote location on the southern peninsula. And then there are 'Jacob's Steps' that return you to the carpark, some 110 metres above Fingal Beach. Take on the challenge.

Start	Fingal Beach Picnic Area, Cape Schanck
Distance	7 kilometres
Time	Minimum 2+ hours, allow up to 4 hours with a group.
Grade	Medium to hard
Map	Melways Map 259 B9
When	Almost anytime, low tide suggested. Avoid this area on Code Red and Total Fire Ban days.

The walk commences at the conspicuous 'Pines' Picnic Area on the Cape Schanck Road. Immediately turn right as you enter the picnic area. There are barbeque facilities with tables, an amenities block and ample space for games. Ensure you are well equipped and prepared for this wild coast walk. There is little protection for the entire length of this walk!

The well-signposted walking track is around 100 metres from the entry point to the park. Walk up the stairs into a forested and well-defined walking track.

This track meets the clifftop track at a T-intersection. Turn right and

Fingal Picnic Area and Beach Circuit.

walk along this scenic pathway. There are glimpses of the ocean and a well-positioned lookout is a worthwhile vantage point which has commanding views of the rugged coastline and ocean 100 metres below. Continue on the track until a junction is reached. Take the right hand path, through the forest to Gunnamatta. This sheltered track parallels the coastline and gradually descends to the beach. On a warm summers' day or with strong winds you will be well protected in here. However, this is not a place to be on a day of extreme fire danger! There is another lookout, about 30 minutes from the start of your walk. This is an excellent location for a break and camera opportunity. There are views towards Gunnamatta and the coastline beyond Point Nepean.

Continue your gradual descent to the beach, passing a small side-track on your left but continuing straight ahead. (This side track may be useful as access in an emergency. It meets the coast half way between

Fingal Beach and your entry point onto the main ocean beach.) Well within the hour you will reach the open foredunes that lead into the beach. Distinctive red-topped marker poles will guide you to the beach. You are now on an exposed, sandy ocean beach, a marked contrast to the sheltered and green forest track.

It does not take long to reach the start of the rocky section on this walk. The sandy foredunes with their distinctive marram grasses give way to sandstone/calcerite cliffs that gradually increase in height and 'power'. There is something awesome about this coastline. Completely untamed, blasted by Bass Strait swell and wind, which is derived from the mighty Southern Ocean. Pause somewhere along this scoured shoreline to take in and appreciate nature at its finest. There are some small headlands to negotiate and small sections of sandy beach will make for a slightly easier journey. Again, take care when walking on any wet rocks. Walking poles and good soled footwear are a wise investment. Take care if there is a strong incoming tide or if you are uncertain about reaching Fingal Beach in safety. It is always prudent to retrace your steps if you are at all concerned about your safety. This is not a coastline with which to take chances. Good pilots, good skippers and good bushwalkers know when to turn back. Even the skipper of the Spirit of Tasmania turned the ship back to Devonport a few years ago … point taken.

As you head closer to Fingal Beach the cliffs are getting higher and the stairway from the beach back to the carpark comes into view. It doesn't take long to reach the steps but it's the slow ascent that will test the fitness of any walker. I would recommend a maximum temperature below 25 degrees for this walk. At times you will find there is little breeze on the slow climb up this long stairway. The wind rolls up and over the 100 metre high cliffs here but it can have surprisingly little effect on the lower reaches of the track. Rest stops are usually required and ensure you have some water left over to quench your thirst.

It is a welcome sight to reach the end of the arduous stairway and take the track that you negotiated earlier in the day. An even more welcome sight is the carpark and your vehicle. Well done.

To extend this walk or change the end point, consider walking through to Gunnamatta with a car rendezvous previously arranged. The beach is wide and sprawling and offers little in the way of shelter. It is the domain of intrepid surf fishermen and keen surfers. The distance to Gunnamatta carpark from the 'Coastal Walk' marker poles which are half way between Fingal Beach and Gunnamatta is less than 2 kilometres.

Take care when hiking close to any shoreline exposed to ocean swell, particularly where your hike will take you close to breaking waves. Please be advised that 'King' waves can occur as frequently as every 2 hours or 1000 waves and that these wave heights can be in the order of up to another 80% of the average wave height*. As mentioned elsewhere, N.S.W. rock fishermen have seen 23 of their number perish over a 24 month period in recent times.

Source: Bureau of Meteorology

FLINDERS JETTY TO WEST HEAD

A short walk with plenty of interest to be found at a commercial jetty. The volcanic rock formations at West Head are a definite must see. Perhaps a lunch at Flinders could be your reward later?

Start	Car park adjacent Flinders Jetty, Flinders
Distance	3 kilometres
Time	Allow
Grade	Easy
Maps	Melways 262 B9
When	Low tide only
Note	Do not attempt this walk with large swell. Rock hopping - solid footwear recommended

This walk commences from the car park at Flinders jetty. This is a popular location for scuba divers, yachties, fishermen and visitors to the area.

Walk along the sandy beach towards the impressive West Head, which is occupied by the Royal Australian Navy. You may encounter mounds of seaweed here and further along the coast near the sailing club loose rocks will need to be negotiated. On a recent midwinter walk I encountered hundreds of silver gulls and perhaps a dozen white-faced heron, a few sooty oyster catchers and 15 to 20 ducks. The solitary ibis seemed to be the exception to the 'safety in numbers 'rule. All

Flinders Jetty to West Head.

these birds seemed to be taking advantage of the relatively calm waters adjacent to the sailing club.

As you pass the sailing club the volcanic rock on which you are walking becomes somewhat flatter and walking past the first small 'headland' or 'point' about 200 metres to the east of the sailing club the small cliffs and rock platform can become impassable at high tide. You will easily spot the distinctive hexagonal columns of volcanic rock which are a standout feature of this walk. The volcanic activity in this location occurred millions of years ago and the rare pink crystal Gmelinite can be found in the area.

Continue walking along the rocks towards West Head. The terrain has changed now, from the bare, small cliffs to a more 'vegetated' environment. Walking this area during the winter, the colours of the coastal scrub were vibrant greens. Look along the high tide line here for any interesting pieces of flotsam and jetsam which may include lost fishing tackle and unusually shaped pieces of driftwood.

Rounding West Head you are now on a rock platform that is far more exposed to swell from Bass Strait and the Southern Ocean. This area of rock platform is often swept clean by wave action. Again, take extreme care here, even at low tide. Large waves can break over these platforms without warning. If you are unsure of the conditions do not venture around the headland. In any case, you can only walk a little further on the more exposed rock platform before your path is halted by the sea. Return the same way back to the jetty, taking in a different perspective of Flinders along the way.

I have always been fascinated by volcanoes and their associated geology. This interest led me to write a book titled: The Walks of the Shipwreck Coast and Volcano Country. BAS Publishing 2010. This book contains information on 60 walks, 34 walks specifically relate to volcanic sites.

To further your exploration of Flinders I suggest tackling the historic

'Flinders Cable Station Walk, almost directly opposite the jetty. This walk ascends the small foreshore cliff to a lookout and Bass Park, where there is a memorial cairn with great views across Westernport Bay and Phillip Island. The Flinders Cable Station Walk, commemorates the establishment, in 1869, of a telegraph station which connected mainland Australia and Tasmania using Morse code. If you add this extra 'sight-seeing' walk to your repertoire allow another 800 metres and 20 minutes.

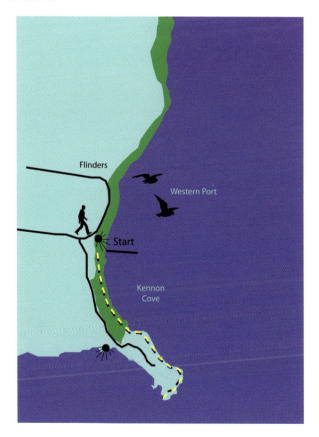

FLINDERS OCEAN BEACH WALK

A superb ocean beach, wind in your hair, wide open spaces. Freedom from the hustle and bustle. Take a short walk on the 'wild side' at one of my favourite locations.

Start	Golf Links Road, Flinders
Distance	Up to 4 kilometres
Time	Allow 1+ hour
Grade	Flat and easy
Maps	Melways map 262 B11, or 261 K10
When	Any time, low tide preferable

This walk commences adjacent to the Royal Australian Navy installation and Pilot Station at West Head. If this first carpark is full, (Eg: during the summer months and with good surfing conditions) you may consider parking at Melways map reference 261 K10, emergency marker MOR503.

Before starting the walk and descending the stairs from the 'Gunnery car park', take in the views from the viewing platform. Once on the beach strike out due west, towards Cape Schanck. There is a sandy beach flanked by small cliffs which gradually diminish in size as you reach the next carpark and the Mushroom Reef Marine Sanctuary, as indicated in your Melways directory.

An informative pamphlet by Parks Victoria titled 'Mushroom Reef Marine Sanctuary gives details of the marine ecosystem and the fact that some animal species discovered here were not previously known

Flinders Ocean Beach.

to science. Recent discoveries include a seastar that broods its young in its stomach!

Continue walking around the small arc of the next 'beach' which is flanked by the Flinders Golf Course*. At low tides the extensive reefs and rock platforms will be exposed here. Despite the daily onslaught of wave action and ocean swell at this location, the outer reefs protect this area and the water is unusually 'calm' close to the shoreline. As you pass a small point or headland the beach changes in character. Many small rock boulders are now apparent. This can make for more difficult walking. A small creek, Double Creek, enters the ocean here. At this point I chose to turn around and leave the Flinders to Cape Schanck section for another day.

An alternative return route worth considering is to head out along King Street to the main road, Cook Street, and visit one of the many cafes and restaurants located here. Walk back to your vehicle via the Esplanade and Golf Links Road. Add 1.5 kilometres to your walking distance and another 20-25 minutes.

*My late grandfather, A.R. (Dick) Martin, a past President of the Victorian Golfing League, won a silver trophy at this golf course many years ago. 'Grandpa' always loved playing at the Flinders course and he used to rave about how fresh the ocean air was at Flinders. The Cape Grim atmospheric monitoring station, situated approximately 250 kilometres to the south, is reputed to have some of the cleanest air in the world. Perhaps Flinders occasionally gets this super clean air too!

Note: Storm damage can result in the closure of beach access stairways and tracks. Use alternative routes as required.

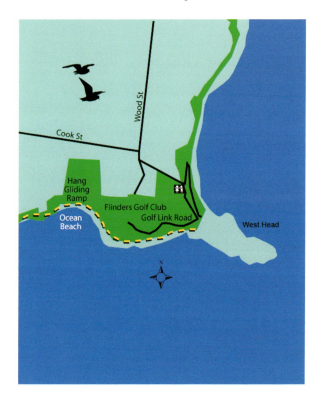

FLINDERS TO CAPE SCHANCK

A challenging cliff-top traverse with impressive views of Bass Strait and the abutting volcanic cliffs make this walk one of the more spectacular on offer on the Mornington Peninsula.

Start	King Street car park Flinders
Distance	14.7 kilometres
Time	Allow five hours. Fast walkers 3.5 hours
Grade	Medium to hard
Maps	Melways 261 H10,
When	Low wind, fine conditions preferred
Suggestion	Wear long pants

Start your walk from a small car park at the southern end of King's Road Flinders. Walk towards a fence and down towards the beach. You will descend some steps as you head towards the beach. Pass the Creek and ascend a small grassy hill, following any well worn track. Pick up the fence line and continue on the mown grassed area. This pathway soon becomes overgrown and you will have to negotiate bracken fern and coastal scrub for a few hundred metres. (Note this part of the walk is unsuitable for small children) Stay close to the fence line as you head towards the Blow Hole. Some of the long grass, spiky weeds and blackberries make for difficult walking. After considerable walking effort, you will reach the Blow Hole. From the Blow Hole pick up the coastal walking track which is wide enough for management vehicles. Walking is considerably easier now, the slowest part of the walk is now

Flinders to Cape Schanck.

behind you. Take the left hand walking track, which is signposted. This descends to a small gully.

Continue walking along the coastal reserve which is part of the Mornington Peninsula National Park. Tea Tree Creek is the next major feature on this part of the walk. This will be easy to locate. You will have to negotiate the fence and walkway as you make your way towards Bushrangers Bay and Cape Schanck.

Cross the small creek and ascend a fairly steep grassed hill, heading again towards the fence line. The grass had been recently mown and made for easy progress. There was a small detour around a dam but otherwise the walking was well paced. I was averaging around 6 kilometres an hour on this much easier section of the walk. As you continue moving forward look behind you to see the spectacular coastline peel away towards Flinders.

After continuing along the coastal reserve you now arrive at the first electric fence and you are now entering private property. Negotiate the stile and continue taking the coastal verge towards Cape Schanck. Permission from property owners should be sought prior to undertaking this section of walk.

There is another very small creek to cross and some longer grass here, however, the walk is still relatively easy. Look behind you to see the distinctive outline of Cape Woolamai in the distance. Along this section of the walk you are 55 metres above the sea. There are rocky boulder beaches to be seen. Steep cliffs with inaccessible sections of coastline are far below.

Some fences run all the way to the cliff edges here and some gates and crossing points are within metres of these cliffs so exercise caution. There is a spectacular and accessible rocky beach along this section of the walk. I chose to walk down to this beach and admire the driftwood which had been stacked neatly into the shape of a beacon. With an offshore wind and a heavy swell surging onto the coast it was a spectacular scene. Climbing out of the cove took some effort and before long I could make out the distinctive forest of Greens Bush to the north west. With a fine and sunny day the Cape Schanck lighthouse, with its distinctive white and red colours, was bathed in sunlight and it reminded me of a similar view towards Cape Liptrap in South Gippsland. Bushrangers Bay starts to loom large as does the distinctive Pulpit Rock at the very tip of Cape Schanck. A solid 11 kilometres of walking will get you to the start of Bushrangers Bay.

Walking from Bushrangers Bay to Cape Schanck car park will present little difficulty on a well maintained national park walking track.

The walk from Cape Schanck to Bushrangers Bay is covered in detail in walk number 12.

If you're exploring the coastline below Cape Schanck please heed the warning sign at the entrance of the car park. 'There are no lifesaving patrols and beware of ocean hazards'.

Note: There may not be continuous mobile phone coverage between Flinders and Cape Schanck. It may be prudent to phone for your chauffeur prior to arriving at Cape Schanck.

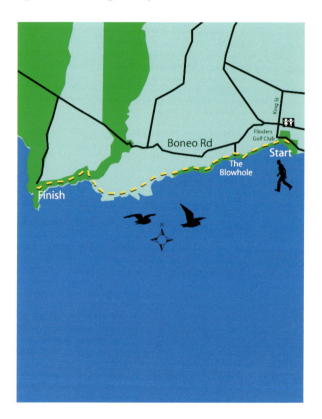

GUNNAMATTA TO BOAGS ROCKS

On this short circuit walk you will experience rugged, sandy ocean beaches, sandstone cliffs and an inland 'fire-break' track which will add another perspective to this 'wild coast' location.

Start	Gunnamatta carpark
Distance	3 kilometres
Time	Under 1 hour
Grade	Easy to medium. Rock-hopping and climbing small sand dunes
Maps	Melways Map 252 D12
When	Anytime. Low tides preferable
Suggestion	Take binoculars

The loop walk may be an appetite builder if you're planning a short visit to Gunnamatta. Leave your vehicle at the first car park at Gunnamatta beach and pick up the signed walking track that heads through the coastal scrub and takes you towards the beach. From the vantage point of the high sand dune just before you descend to the beach, take in the rolling and stunning coastline towards Cape Schanck. The Cape Schanck Lighthouse will be visible, perched high above this prominent headland.

Follow the coastal walk signs and head along the beach in a North-westerly direction towards the rocks. Take note of this sensitive shore bird habitat and any advisory signs displayed by Parks Victoria. Also

Coastline near Boags Rocks.

take note of the warning signs near the sandstone cliffs and caves. Tragically some beach goers who sheltered under similar unstable sandstone at Margaret River in Western Australia did not go home.

As you walk on to some higher ground perhaps to avoid the lower traverse which has much rock hopping, you should notice the remains of the many aboriginal middens which are scattered throughout the entire point Nepean National Park. The walk towards Boags Rocks is a mixture of small sandy coves flanked by sandstone cliffs and some shallow caves. There may be numerous large stands of bubble weed washed up high on the shoreline. What is more unusual here, is to see bull kelp on the beach. King Island, which lies approximately 140 kilometres to the southwest, has so much bull kelp washing up on its coastline that there is a whole industry devoted to its collection, drying and processing for export overseas.

As you approach the Boags Rocks outfall there is more rock hopping on loose, small rocks before you reach the sealed road. This road, which cuts through the fore dune, takes you back to Truemans Road. Not walking track signage to your left as you leave the coast. This walking track takes you to St Andrews and Rye ocean beaches. Rye Ocean Beach carpark is under 3 kilometres away. The wide management vehicle track, is not particularly scenic but is very serviceable. Once you have reached Truemans road I would advise that you walk on the side of the road back to the car park. The more appealing horse trail, which winds its way through the coastal scrub, is very narrow with insufficient room for walkers and horses at any one time.

On high tides or heavy swell keep well away from the water's edge and watch out for surging waves that can come higher onto the beach. Do

Sand dunes near Boags Rocks.

not take any chances particularly with young children. There are many warning signs around the Gunnamatta precinct. This is one of most dangerous beaches along the Australian coastline. Some years ago a family came here on a summer's day and tragically not all returned home. If you must swim, please swim between the flags but also know your own capabilities. The R.A.C.V. has recommended people not swim along the coastline from Cape Schanck to Point Nepean. This is my general rule of thumb too. T.V. programs such as Bondi Rescue indicate that many people will go for a swim without the knowledge or swimming ability needed for particular conditions or locations. Again, children must be closely and fully supervised, continuously, along this section of coast.

And with three walkers lost within a month in Victoria in the winter of 2011 and only one returning home, we undertook this walk with full safety gear, including a personal locator beacon and lightweight, compact personal flotation devices as well is the usual hiking requisites. They say most motor vehicle accidents happen close to home. Could it be also true that most bushwalking incidents either occur close to home or where we have become seemingly all-too-familiar with the location and terrain. Proceed with caution. On a winter solstice day with a very cold onshore winds and air temperature of around 12° the wind chill

must have been around 5°C. Rain squalls were scudding in from Bass Strait and this necessitated a spray coat, gloves and a beanie.

There is the option to extend this walk and finish your trek at St Andrews Beach or the Rye Ocean Beach car park which around 4.5 kilometres to the northwest.

25

HASTING FORESHORE RESERVE

Lots to see, a good quality walking track with an extensive boardwalk which passes extensive stands of mangroves. The Hastings Yacht Club, jetty and the Pelican Park Recreation Centre and café all combine to make this an enjoyable walk with a difference.

Start	Hastings Jetty car park,
Distance	7 kilometres return
Time	90 minutes
Effort	Easy to medium.
Maps	Melways map 154 K11
When	High tide and a sunny day

This is a busy precinct. With the ever-popular jetty, nearby boat ramp and recreation centre which includes a heated pool, I have never seen this location without people. Pelicans are usually an attendance at this location and there may be the possibility of buying bird feed to give to the ever hungry pelicans. Before setting off on this walk, take time to read the information board opposite the Pelican Pantry Café.

As you commence your walk from the start of the jetty, head in a northerly direction. You will quickly move away from the centre of all the activity. The path passes some bollards and soon enough there is a more relaxed pace and feel to the walk. Expansive playing fields, strategically placed trees and a foreshore of mangroves all add to the experience. There are good views to the east and French Island as well as Long Island Point.

Hastings Jetty.

The well-maintained path, which is also used by cyclists, is easy to follow. Keep bearing right at any of the path intersections to arrive at the start of a long board walk. This will take you across Kings Creek and into Babington Park which is the turn-around point for this walk. Return the same way or for some variation bear right at any of the track intersections, still keeping on the coastal side of Marine Parade, to arrive at your starting point.

The Hastings foreshore reserve is a wonderful community asset with a playground and tennis club. The well-placed seats along part of this walk may also prove useful. The walk and track is suitable for strollers and young children with bikes. This location has an amenities block as well as barbeques.

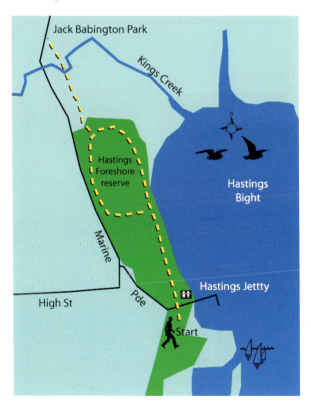

JACKS BEACH RESERVE TO HASTINGS

26

An easy and straightforward walk, almost impossible to get lost and with hundreds of meters of boardwalk to speed you on your way. This is a peaceful location with some history as well as signage highlighting the fauna and flora of the area.

Start	Jacks Beach Reserve, Bittern
Distance	6 kilometres return
Time	2 hours return
Effort	Easy, flat.
Maps	Melways map 165 A7
When	Anytime
Suggestion	Take binoculars

There is ample parking at the reserve, where there is an amenities block and barbeque facilities. Follow the path towards Hastings and then take the right hand track at the T- intersection which takes you out to Jacks Beach and a tanning pit used by some of the Jack family to tan their cotton fishing nets. From this beach you may be able to see the Oberon class submarine, the Otama, moored in Westernport Bay.

Retrace your steps, heading roughly due west on a well-formed gravel path. Within a few hundred metres you will start on the extensive board walk which will have you 'skimming' over the top of the Westernport Bay mangroves towards Hastings. The wide, timbered boardwalk, which is well over a kilometre in length, is a very different walk to the majority of treks available to walkers on the Mornington Peninsula.

Jack Brothers Tan Pit.

The extensive mangrove vegetation here protects the shoreline and is in marked contrast to the Port Phillip Bay coastline and the scoured ocean beaches from Flinders to Point Nepean.

Detailed signage en route gives the walker a better appreciation of this complex ecosystem, which at first sight does not appear to be as productive and important to planet earth as first impressions would indicate. The mangroves here comprise 10% of the Western Port Bay shoreline. The mangroves are habitat for many nesting, roosting and feeding shore birds and migratory birds. This area is listed under the RAMSAR Convention and bird species here include black swans, golden plovers, ibis, stints and pelicans.

Some of the food sources for these birds include juvenile fish and crustaceans who also make this amazing ecosystem their home.

When you reach a lookout point, marked in your Melways Directory, you will have elevated views of the surrounding area and this is an obvious photographic point too. As you move along the boardwalk towards Salmon Street, the residential development of Hastings becomes prominent and the Westernport Marina looms large. Follow the foreshore walking path until you reach the marina. I personally like to inspect all things 'nautical in nature' so I always make a bee-line for boats and moorings. The marina here is no exception. After perusing the boats, rescue craft, yachts and charter vessels it is time to return to the start of your walk, by simply retracing your steps.

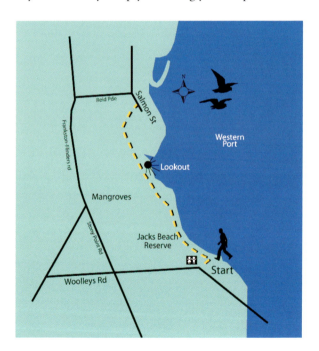

KANGERONG NATURE CONSERVATION RESERVE

Easy walking through a less well-known reserve. This area is popular with birdwatchers. This is only one of two reserves found on the 'Red Hill' red clay. Come and investigate for yourself.

Start	McIlroys Road Red Hill
Distance	750 metres, loop
Time	20 minutes
Effort	Very easy
Map	Melways map 191 E1
When	Anytime except Code Red days

The starting point is approximately 1 kilometre from Red Hill Road. There is very limited parking on a grass verge with only enough room for three vehicles.

Commencing your walk at emergency marker NPP 504 follow the track as it winds it way through a delightful forest. The track is relatively flat as it parallels the 'river' flats abutting Dunns Creek. After 500 metres the track swings to a southerly direction, with a slight rise. I heard the distinctive thumps of a kangaroo or wallaby making its way through the bush.

Presently you will walk up towards McIlroy Road and a fence line the before walking out onto the road itself and returning to your vehicle. Short in duration, easy to navigate and definitely less frequented than many of the more popular spots on the peninsula.

While a track is very navigable it was somewhat overgrown and with

113

Kangerong Nature Reserve.

young children in your party I would make sure they are at the rear of the group as this walk is near a creek and snakes may certainly be present during the summer months. There was a noticeable presence of a variety of sounds of birds during early autumn when I walked at this location. Keen bird observers would no doubt be able to identify many of the calls heard in this area of bushland.

There is a website which has recorded many of the more common bird calls found on the Mornington Peninsula and this may be of interest to those who have completed this walk. See www.birdsaustralia.com.au, the Birds Australia website, to hear various bird calls. This may also be of interest to younger people and children in your walking group.

114

KINGS FALLS

An interesting, short walk and perfect introduction for first-time walkers. Kings Falls has numerous vegetation types from grass trees, she-oaks and stands of impressive eucalypts to native pines and grasses. There are many information signs to add interest and keep you in the right direction. Lookouts give commanding views of the nearby scenery.

Start	Waterfall Gully Road, Main Ridge
Distance	1 km
Time	30+ minutes
Grade	Easy, steps
Maps	Melways Map 171 D5
When	Preferably in winter and spring after rain
Note	Avoid Total Fire Ban days

Come away from the busier precincts of the peninsula and arrive at an altogether more sedate and relaxing location. Drive down the gravelled Waterfall Gully Road for one and a half kilometres to arrive at the signposted walk and car parking area. There is a good walking track to follow and you're away on an adventure.

King's Waterfall loop is a short, easy round trip that will not tax even the occasional walker. This small waterfall flows throughout the year and different vegetation types can be seen along the way. Fern gullies, dry eucalypt forest, casurinas (she-oaks) and grass trees, as well as the impressive scrambling coral fern all add to the interest of this walk. It is worthwhile to note that the grass trees can grow to be a few hundred years in age.

Kings Falls.

This route takes in some spectacular bay views as well as Port Phillip Heads. Some of the views across one of the ridges and out towards the Bellarine Peninsula give the walker that 'wilderness feeling'. You seem to be many kilometres from civilization and there are no houses or roads in sight. It is interesting to note that some of the vegetation on this track has never been cleared for farming as the terrain was too difficult for farmers to cultivate.

There are numerous information signs along this track, which cover some of the aspects of this section of the park. The track is well maintained for most of its length and shade is provided along much of the route by eucalypts and other forest vegetation.

King's Falls cascades over some of the exposed granite, which forms part of the bedrock in this area. Note the unusual brown granite here, which is a hallmark of the Arthurs Seat geology. There is a lookout at the falls and impressive views of the steep and thickly forested gully may make this a good location for camera enthusiasts. A stop at the falls could well be a pleasant place for a picnic.

For those wanting to extend their walk, there is the option of heading out towards Seawinds, near the summit of Arthur's Seat for a car rendezvous, or to head down the mountain towards Carrington Park. Either way you will add about 1 kilometre to your walk and another 20 minutes one way. You may also choose to hike along the walking track from Seawinds to King's Waterfall. Note: the area around Arthur's Seat has numerous cafes and restaurants as well as an interesting car museum on Purves Road. This walk takes in the Arthur's Seat State Park and additional information as well as a map can be obtained by reading the Parks Victoria 'Park Notes' on the 'Arthurs Seat State Park'. This leaflet has three other walks which may be of interest.

KOONYA OCEAN BEACH TO SORRENTO OCEAN BEACH

A walk with great views, a well maintained track and a halfway point where you can obtain the obligatory coffee, lunch or cool drink at Sorrento Ocean Beach. This walk is very popular in the summer months but locals and those with holiday homes use it throughout the year. Come and see why. Take your camera!

Start	Koonya Ocean beach car park, Hughes Road, Blairgowrie
Distance	6 kilometres
Time	2 hours return
Grade	Medium
Maps	Melways Map 166 K2
When	Anytime except Code Red days

This is a great circuit walk to Sorrento using tracks in the Mornington Peninsula National Park. Coppins Track forms part of this very popular walk. Initially, on the cliff tops there are rough walking tracks which skirt around the cliffs but from Diamond Bay to Sorrento Ocean Beach, you will utilize the main walking track. Your return from Sorrento is on the more substantial and signposted pathway to the lower car park adjacent to the amenities block at Koonya Ocean Beach. The return journey is not as scenic in the later stages of the walk but there is the option to climb St Pauls Lookout for another commanding view.

Start this adventurous and challenging walk by heading down to the

Koonya Ocean Beach.

sandy Koonya Beach from the top car park above the amenities block. Head in a north westerly direction along Koonya Beach towards Sorrento. There is a relatively steep rise at the end of the beach and the foot track from the beach is not well signposted, but you will invariably see a well worn path way which takes you on a scenic route to your destination.

As you ascend from Koonya Ocean Beach to a high vantage point you will see the water storage tanks at Sorrento and the very distinctive outline of Coppins Lookout. Keep up high on a roughly formed track and keep well back from the edge of the cliffs. Some sand stone stacks come into view and the sand dune seems to slide all the way to the cliffs edge. Keep well back from the cliff edges as the warning signs advise.

You are now heading out towards a board walk and a railed observation deck. Now continue on the board walk and track, bearing right as you approach a T intersection. The left hand route takes you to Diamond Bay beach, which may be the perfect place for a stop on a hot summer day. From Diamond Bay follow the track which now is closer to the ocean, and in due course you will arrive at Sorrento Ocean Beach. The scenic track eventually meanders its way to the car park at Sorrento Ocean Beach. There is one final pedestrian crossing to negotiate before you enter the Sorrento Ocean Beach precinct. This is the home of the Sorrento Surf Lifesaving Club where the author patrolled for a number of seasons. The beach here, as well as the café, are good reasons for a break before continuing back to Koonya Ocean Beach.

The return journey initially retraces your path back along Coppins Track, passing St Pauls Beach car park and then Jubilee Point turnoff. Continue straight ahead, passing the Diamond Bay car park and back towards Koonya and Hughes Road. Allow up to an hour each way.

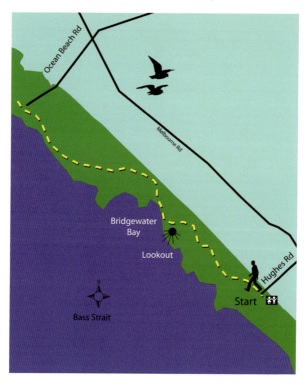

LANGWARRIN FLORA AND FAUNA RESERVE

Here is an amazing reserve that contains nearly half of all the plant species found on the Mornington Peninsula as well as nearly 100 species of birds. There is a considerable historical background here although little remains of the former military establishment. A 'little desert' experience and the substantial views from the northern section make exploration of Langwarrin Reserve very worthwhile.

Start	McCelland Road. Main Entrance
Distance	5 kms or less, circuit
Time	Under 2 hours
Grade	Easy to medium
Maps	Melways Map 103 C10 Parks Vic, Park Notes Langwarrin Flora and Fauna Reserve
When	Anytime subject to weather conditions. Avoid Code Red Days
Suggestion	Take binoculars for bird watching

This paseo (leisurely stroll or walk) lends itself to a circuit walk which selects the more interesting tracks and walking paths, avoiding some of the more mundane firebreak roads.

The well signposted turnoff from McClelland Road has room for about 20 vehicles. There is an excellent information board which details the extensive flora and fauna of this area. Koalas, Brown Bandicoots and Swamp Wallabies are known to frequent the reserve. Stringybarks

Langwarrin Flora and Fauna Reserve.

comprise the main species of tree in the reserve. Swamp Gum, Narrow-leaf Peppermint and Manna Gum also occur. Just as interesting is the former site's history, being used as a military establishment which goes back nearly one hundred years. The Langwarrin Military Reserve was variously used for military exercises involving over 2000 troops and as a prisoner of war camp and a military hospital.

Start your walk by picking up the McClelland 'break' or track which heads in a northerly direction towards the Telstra Depot. We are heading towards the Dune Track which is clearly indicated on the maps. This is a great circuit walk which reminds me of the sunset country in north western Victoria and the Little Desert. With the extremely wet winter of 2011, parts of the McClelland track had been inundated and required some side tracking along the fence line to avoid the water lying in great puddles. Pick up the Telstra boundary fence and head in an easterly direction until you reach the dune track, which is a walking 'only' track. In early spring there were many wildflowers including clematis, wattles, acacia and heaths, to name a few. Soon there is a signposted fork in the track. Take the right hand track, where you will gain some elevation. From the high point of this track there are views of the city skyline, the Dandenong Ranges far to the north and to the south views of the extensive nature of this reserve. Perhaps on a clear day part of Strzelecki Ranges may be visible. The scrub here is quite dense in places with some low eucalypt trees and plenty of audible evidence of the abundant bird life.

Shortly there is another fork in the track. Take the right hand track which heads roughly east then southwest in direction. You are heading towards the Reservoir Track. There is evidence of recent wildfire which reminds us to avoid these areas on days of total fire ban and code red days. One particular eucalypt overhangs the walking track and has the parasitic mistletoe thriving on its host. There was ample evidence of white heath nearby and telltale signs of bull ant activity on the track possibly to remind us to take a first aid kit and also to warn smaller children in our party of the dangers. Another vantage point comes into view and there are glimpses of Port Phillip Bay. Be sure to take the well worn walking tracks and check your navigation en route. During the warmer months snakes will be active.

The Owen Dawson track is clearly signposted and eventually takes you across the Long Crescent management vehicle or 4WD track. Continue until you meet the Stringy Bark Track some half a kilometre to the east. The trees here a somewhat higher and there is substantial leaf litter from the eucalyptus and acacias. A thicket of sedges also makes for a variation on the surrounding vegetation. At this point a substantially sized tree had fallen across the track and as I attempted to negotiate the obstacle, ended up on my rear end almost in the blink of an eye. Take care when walking, particularly in wet or slippery conditions and expect the unexpected. You will pass an orange track marker, the track now starting to descend and you will see a derelict water tank from the days of the military occupation. Notice, large diameter bullet holes which have peppered this object during target practice. Cross the Long Crescent Track and continue in an easterly direction in more open country with lots of bracken fern, acacias in flower, white heath with the occasional pink heath. Ample evidence of moss together with some toadstools highlighted the moister parts of this walk. There is a wooden seat in this section of the track which is sheltered by a large native pine.

Smaller versions of our native grass trees are also to be seen in this part of the walk. This variety of grass tree has a distinctively narrower and shorter spear and smaller diameter 'leaves'. Turn right into the Stringy Bark Track, a wide track used by management vehicles. You will pass the very wide Centre Break track. Continue walking over the Centre Break track into the Aqueduct track. There is a second wooden seat nearby and this may be a perfect excuse for a short stop. This part of the walk continues for over a kilometre until you arrive at a junction with the Paperbark Track. While I did not see many birds on my most recent visit, flame robins and blue wrens did add a splash of colour to the vibrant greens of the early spring growth. Signs of burn-off activities are evident as you approach the Military Track. Navigation through this area of the reserve is relatively straightforward, the vegetation changing again as you approach the main entrance area. Take a photocopy of the park map for optimal navigation.

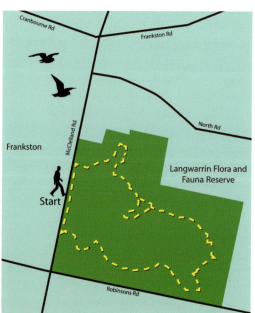

LATROBE RESERVE, DROMANA

Short on distance but big on views, steep at first but easy walking overall. The Latrobe Reserve Scenic Walkway and Link offers a variety of flora and fauna in a relatively small area. Views include Phillip Bay and the Melbourne city skyline.

Start	Point Nepean Road, opposite Anthony's Nose boat ramp
Distance	Up to 2 kilometres return
Time	30+ minutes
Effort	Medium
Maps	Melways Map 159 D8
When	Anytime

The start of this walk is well signposted, with informative signage highlighting interesting facts about the local history as well as a clear map of the immediate area. The leaflet box was empty on my last visit and I would suggest a visit to the Dromana Visitor Information to obtain the very informative leaflet titled, 'Latrobe Reserve'. Named after Victoria's first Superintendent, Charles Latrobe, Governor of Victoria from 1851 to 1854, it is said that Latrobe would visit his good friends, the McCrae's at their homestead, nearby.

Start your ascent from the roadway by negotiating some large steps. Fortunately, the steep grade does not last for very long and within a few minutes the track changes direction and gradient and becomes far more 'walker friendly'. There is a strategically placed seat at the top of this first part of the walk. Glimpses of the bay give the walker a taste

125

Boat ramp and foreshore at Anthonys Nose.

of what is in store when more elevation is gained. Within a few more minutes, Latrobe Parade is reached. Now follow the road towards Foord Lane

On a clear day there are great views towards Mt. Macedon, the city skyline (due north), Mt. Martha and the Mt Dandenong. There is a second, duplicated, information board and leaflet box at the Latrobe Parade exit/entry point. From here walk roughly southwest, paralleling Latrobe Parade and turn into Foord Street, noting the communication towers on Arthurs Seat. Stunning views towards Rosebud Beach, Rosebud Jetty and the historic McCrae lighthouse can be glimpsed through the trees at end of Foord Street. Port Phillip Heads is usually discernable in the distance on a clear day. Allow 20 minutes to end of Foord Street and around half an hour for the round trip.

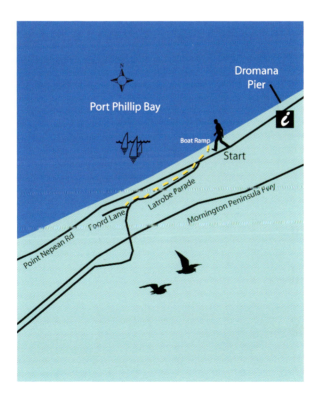

LONG POINT, CAPE SCHANCK

A surprisingly enjoyable walk, initially uninspiring until you walk into the renowned Greens Bush and the eucalypt and bracken fern forest. You may also be lucky enough to see wallabies in residence here. Tread quietly!

Start	End, Long Point Road, Cape Schanck
Distance	4.5 kilometres
Time	1+ hour
Effort	Medium
Maps	Melways map 259 G3
When	Weekdays and except Code Red days

Park adjacent to the Rosebud and District Motorcycle Club entrance. As the bike club is in full swing over the weekends my suggestion is to walk during the week. Cross the bike barrier and follow walking track through a treed forest track, the path being sandy in places but easy to navigate.

The entry to the national park and Greens Bush is impossible to miss, gated and signposted. There is also an information shelter. Continue along the management vehicle track, due east, on the wide fire break.

Signage now indicates the Long Point Circuit Walk is 3.7 kilometres. A map of Greens Bush indicates your position. Continue walking, passing emergency marker MOR565 with bracken fern and acacia trees the dominant vegetation.

There is a T intersection with another 4WD track. Look to your right to see the communication towers at Arthurs Seat.

Long Point.

The track now descends and there are pastures in the distance, beyond Main Creek. Two Bays Walking Track is passed and you continue straight ahead to the old campsite and Main Creek. The descent is not steep and on the last walk there were many roo and wallaby tracks.

The track now flattens out and bears to the south east, then south and finally terminates in a flat, grassed area, the warning sign reading: 'Danger Falling Limbs'.

Walk back out to the Two Bays Walking Track intersection. Turn left onto a true bushwalking track, narrower, far more pleasant and intimate. You are instantly more at one with nature. The weather on this winters' day was 14C and overcast with very light rain. You will pass a wooden seat with views across the gully and towards the distant farming land. The walk meanders through the forest, the track being very flat here. There is a short board walk over a creek with a few ferns and half a dozen steps to tackle on the far side. In this particular area, during the damp winter months, the trunks of the eucalypts have a yellowish covering of fine lichen which is rather unusual.

Another seat comes into view and within 10 metres there is a T-intersection which is well signposted. Rogers Road at 1.5 kilometres distance is your destination. Walk under a mistletoe which has attached itself to an over-hanging eucalypt. Look for a smaller variety of bracken fern as you walk along this section of track. It is noticeably lighter green in colour, with a more delicate leaf and a lower height profile. While there was some wind in the tops of the trees, the forest floor is well protected here and almost completely calm.

On the third leg of this walk the narrow path, the eucalypt and bracken fern forest and the sighting of two wallabies within 50 metres of each other was a real treat. These forest dwellers were not at all worried by my presence and continued to stay in one spot while I took some photos. The track continues to wind its way through the bush and a clearing allows views across a small valley to the south. There is another seat. Six or seven rosellas make their presence heard as I continue walking and then the track turns to a more northerly bearing. A slow gradual rise is apparent but still within most peoples capabilities. The path eventually meets the main firebreak and management vehicle track which you walked on earlier in the day. Now continue back to your vehicle.

At the commencement of this walk I wondered why I was walking at this venue. With noisy motor bikes and an uninspiring, wide vehicle track and fire break, the location did not get me in the right walking mood. But this walk got better with every step. It was absolutely delightful and I'll be back very soon. The forest beyond awaits.

Having led bushwalks for over 20 years, a first aid kit is always handy. On this walk I was solo as my partner was sleeping in after a late shift.

I took some comfort knowing that my EPIRB was on board. With no mobile coverage even the UHF radio could prove useful in an emergency. Take care.

Be fully prepared for any eventuality.

33

MAIN CREEK WALK

A relaxing venue and a very short walk. Just the thing before a lunch break. Come and experience a peaceful part of the Mornington Peninsula National Park.

Start	Main Creek picnic area, Boneo Road
Distance	640 metres
Time	15 minutes
Effort	Easy, some steps
Maps	Melways map 260 A9
When	Anytime

The picnic tables beckon and with limited parking for just a few vehicles you will be away from the crowds. Perhaps you will be the only group here to enjoy the location all by yourselves.

This loop walk is well within everyones' capabilities and it is easy to follow. When I tackled this walk in late autumn Main Creek had an excellent water flow, 'babbling away' as the watercourse made its way to Bushrangers Bay, approximately 2 kilometres to the south west. The track winds its way past a high point close to the creek where there is a good vantage point overlooking this water course. The track was very well maintained with mown grass for the most part of the walk. There are a few steps which take you to a point about 20 metres above the Main Creek. Again, another good vantage for a photographic opportunity. For the return journey the track skirts alongside Boneo Road and within a few short minutes you will have returned to the start of your walk. Now it's time to have lunch or afternoon tea or coffee.

Main Creek.

During the winter months the mown grass track may have sufficient moisture to saturate any lightweight footwear. This is what I found on my last walk through here. Carrying a spare pair of shoes is always a good idea as you have dry footwear for the vehicle return journey and as well, putting on different footwear after a walk can be like putting on slippers. Try it for yourself, especially after a long walk.

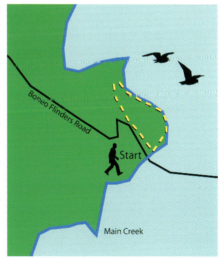

MAIN RIDGE NATURE CONSERVATION RESERVE

34

A circuit walk through a picturesque and tranquil reserve. Bulrushes and tree ferns are found here and maiden hair fern will also be observed during most months of the year.

Start	Mornington-Flinders Road, Main Ridge, 1 kilometre south of Shands Rd
Distance	Around 3 kilometres
Time	1 hour loop walk
Effort	Easy, undulating
Maps	Melways Map 255 C4, Parknotes: Northern Peninsula Parks and Reserves, Visitor Guide, Parks Victoria. www.parkweb.vic.gov.au/resources
When	Any time except Code Red days

There are two walker entry points accessed from the Mornington-Flinders Road, approximately one kilometre south of Shands Road at Main Ridge. There is limited parking space here but additional parking can be located off Barkers Road.

I commenced walking from the Bakers Road entry. Notice evidence of previous wildfire in this reserve. This is a tranquil area of the peninsula and the walk is also enjoyable for its desolation. Take the right hand grassed vehicle track, which slowly descends towards the eastern boundary of the park. At another junction, indicated by a blue-arrowed marker post, veer left again, into a wide walking track which will take you through a stand of bracken fern.

Kangaroo Paw Fern.

The larger eucalypts in this part of the reserve have tapped into the water table, being the headwaters of Mantons Creek, which flows into Westernport Bay. Having descended from the high point of the reserve, you now head towards a magnificent stand of tree ferns, interdispersed with rushes, which form part of a creek bed. The track narrows appreciably here and becomes a true walking path, with wooden footbridges to bypass the dampest parts of this marshy area.

Tree ferns here are over 2 metres in height, and are always impressive, particularly when you consider that they only grow at the rate of 30mm per year. During the damp months delicate maidenhair ferns will be noticeable on this section of the track. The track now ascends towards the western entrance and before long intersects with the old asphalt roadway. From here, bear left until you return to the start of your walk.

There is a hollow trunk of a massive gum tree right beside the walking track. Although suffering from the effects of wildfire, there appears to be a healthy upper canopy of foliage for this giant of the forest. Note that parts of the track can become muddy in the winter months but overall the track is in very good condition.

Also notice the large sawn eucalypt tree stump on your right. Last century my father-in-law remembers that there was a timber mill located in these parts but now very few signs of that former activity are visible. This short walk would be an ideal introduction for younger walkers.

When you have completed your trek why not consider visiting Sunny Ridge Strawberry Farm, a little over 2 kilometres away? With over 300,000 visitors every year, this is a venue not to be missed. Peak times are from December to February but try March to May visits for easier access.

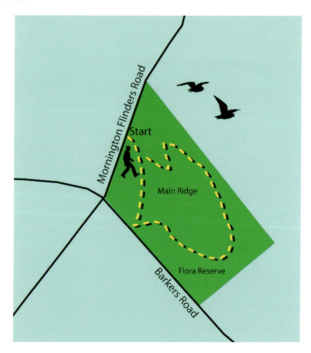

MAIN RIDGE TO CAPE SCHANCK

Come and experience part of the famous Two Bays walking track. There is solitude and relaxation for the walker while viewing magnificent stands of eucalypt forests, fern glades and impressive areas of grass trees as well as heathlands and grasslands. Grey kangaroos inhabit this area and wildflowers including the pink heath and acacias are all on show at various times of the year.

Start	Browns Road and Hyslops Road, Rosebud
Distance	Up to 16 kilometres return
Time	Up to 5 hours
Effort	Medium
Maps	Parks Victoria: Parknotes Greens Bush, Melways 171 B11
When	Any time but avoid forests on Code Red days
Suggestion	Organise a car shuttle. Shorter walk options are available

The main trek is a 'long-haul' walk for keen, well-equipped and fit walkers. However, this walk also readily lends to shorter hikes that will suit people with less time on their hands.

Start your walk at either of two places.

The first start, for a longer walk, is at the intersection of Browns and Hyslops Roads. Walk along this gravel country 'lane' for approximately

2 kilometres until the end of the road. Continue through the wooden barrier, notice the advisory sign regarding cinnamon fungus, and head towards Limestone Road.

The shorter walk could commence at the end of Hyslops Road, saving walkers 1.8 kilometres and perhaps 20 to 30 minutes.

Immediately leaving my vehicle I was aware of the many birds that inhabit the area as well as the peacefulness of this location. Wind in the trees, clouds scudding across the sky. 'At one with nature', as they say.

From Limestone Road it is 1.6 km to Greens Bush. Walk along the Limestone Road for a few metres to the well signposted track heading towards Greens Bush. This track is your traditional bush walking track, narrow and single file but well maintained, with a good 'bushy' feel. Walk past emergency marker MOR619. A delightful eucalypt forest can be found here. You have well and truly left civilisation behind and your journey into the wilderness continues. Further along the track you come into an area with extensive grass tree coverage. Excellent seasonal rain should produce many grass tree 'spears' in the lead up to summer. Passing another management vehicle track, continue along this route. The walking trail is relatively flat until it makes the gradual descent to Lightwood Creek.

While re-walking this track in May of 2011 I dropped my map 'somewhere along the path.' Fortunately I had to re-trace my steps for only a short distance, some 70 metres, to last stopping point, before finding the map. But another lesson is learned. I've lost maps before. In Bass Strait, on Flinders Island, a map literally blew away in the gusty wind. The lesson is clear. Attach your map to a lanyard and place it in a waterproof pocket.

Another road and intersection will appear. Greens Bush is 300 metres distant and it is 8.3 kilometres to Boneo Road. With 1.8 kilometres to Baldry Crossing, this featured walk could be tackled on another

Greens Bush.

day. There is a small boardwalk over a minor creek. Emergency marker MOR 562 appears. The track is still very well maintained and signposted so you should have no trouble navigating your way towards the coast. Presently you will walk into a gully with lots of fern fronds. The track now takes a more westerly direction and you will find yourself walking through a bracken fern thicket between two sections of forest. There are glimpses of views towards Bass Strait, these being the only views of the coast on this particular section of the walk until you come closer to Bushrangers Bay.

There is now a gradual descent towards Lightwood Creek. A small boardwalk and sign will be found here with a large stand of tree ferns. This part of the walk then starts to skirt along Main Creek which eventually heads out towards Boneo Road.

Another management 4WD track, well maintained and wide will present itself.

The entire section of this 'Two Bays Walk' has an excellent track and is generally far superior to the Arthurs Seat to Browns Road section. The track was surprisingly dry, given that the previous day experienced drizzle for most of the day.

The occasional wooden seat along this track may be a welcome spot to have a rest. As you approach Boneo Road you will hear the distinctive sound of traffic. I found this comforting in as much as I knew that I was approaching my rendezvous point. (I had arranged to leave my mountain bike at the Bushrangers Bay carpark with the intention to ride up to Long Point Road and to head back towards Rogers Road and into Limestone Road. I would not advise you to take this route. It took me around one and a half hours to get back to the car.)

Main Ridge to Cape Schanck.

Just a few metres before Boneo Road there is a substantial sign indicating the contribution of the Greens family to the Greens Bush and also information on the impact of cinnamon fungus.

At Boneo Road you can continue on towards Cape Schanck, via Bushrangers Bay. Pick up the signposted Bushrangers Bay track. This Track slowly descends towards the coast and you will gain great views of the coastline and the small sandy beach on your approach. There are more pronounced stands of coastal 'Banksia and more open forest than the compact forests found at Long Point and Greens Bush. This section of the Two Bays walk has much cleared farmland, which distracts from an otherwise excellent bushwalk. From Bushrangers Bay track Junction, pick up the path to Cape Schanck, which is written up in walk number 12.

Again, this walk is very well signposted, being one of the two major walks on the peninsula. Before undertaking this hike you and your party need to consider the logistics.

Fast walkers or those undertaking a training regime may be able to walk the route between the end of Hyslops Road and Boneo Road in around two hours with short stops.

MARTHA POINT, PEBBLE BEACH, MT MARTHA

A surprisingly remote part of the bay can be found around Martha Point. Brown granites, sometimes adorned with stunning with orange lichen, offer a challenge to the hardy walker. This is rock-hopping at its best.

Start	Car park opposite Ellerina Road, Mt Martha
Distance	2 kilometres return
Time	Allow at least one hour
Effort	Medium, flat but almost continual rock-hopping
Maps	Melways Map150 D9
When	Low tide only, under 0.5 metres preferred
Suggestion	Well soled hiking footwear. Suit experienced walkers. Walking poles may be useful.

Here is a walk that requires some preparation. Ensure you take the usual hiking requisites. The sandy, sleepy and laid-back bay beaches from Dromana to Portsea are in stark contrast to the almost continuous rocky shoreline along this cliffy part of the peninsula. More than this, the desolation and relatively peaceful nature of location here make this walk very different. The walk is no Sunday stroll. Almost every step requires concentration but this is part of the challenge. Attempting this walk at high tide may result in your progress being halted by cliffs.

Entry into Pebble Beach is well sign-posted from the southern end of the small carpark near the intersection of Marine Parade and Ellerina Road. There is a small amount of sand at Pebble Beach, but the name

View of Safety Beach from Pebble Beach.

says it all. There is more rock than pebbles. The walking is easy for the first part of this trek. The granitic rocks are reminiscent of King and Flinders Islands in Bass Strait. If you are observant you may see twin-engined aircraft plying the King Island route as they pass reasonably close to Martha Point.

(See 'The Walks of King Island' by the same author.)

There are some small rock pools with pretty necklace seaweed to distract your attention. Small rock pools can be a microcosm of life. About Martha Point itself the ribbon seaweeds are more obvious. As you traverse the shoreline look above the high water mark for interesting pieces of otsam and jetsam, particularly after heavy weather.

The further you walk towards Martha Point the slower the pace becomes, with larger rocks to negotiate. You will encounter small gutters

Search & Rescue at Martha Point.

and rock ledges which require an assessment as to which way will be the easiest 'track' to take. On a few sections of the trek you may find it easier to climb up onto the higher part of the rocky coastline before coming back down to the smoother, lower part of the shoreline. Take extra care when walking over wet rocks.

Rounding Martha Point there are even more difficult sections of rock to traverse. A derelict rail track with some old cement reinforcement is in evidence nearby. Before long you will gain uninterrupted views of the city skyline and the coastline towards Mt Martha village and Mornington. At this point I decided to have a lunch break before retracing my steps back to my vehicle.

Note that the buoys to the south and seaward here delineate the mussel farm area.

It is highly recommended that you have suitable footwear for this hike. Light weight hiking boots, cross trainers or runners with good tread are essential for good grip over the rocks and also to cushion your feet from walking over rough terrain.

An interesting scene was played out at this location when I last did this walk in early 2011. A group of three friends had decided to walk along the coastline here. Having come from Bradford Road they decided to take a short cut and scale the cliffs back to Marine Parade. One of their party became stuck on the almost sheer cliff face and the Police Air Wing was called in to winch a young male to safety. A lesson learnt. Judging from the lack of hiking equipment carried by the other two 'walkers', one might assume they were inexperienced hikers. The lessons are clear. Know your capabilities. Don't take unnecessary risks and walk with ample equipment including, water, coat, first aid kit, etc.

For a longer walk, depart from the northern side of the Martha Cove marina tunnel entrance.

MORNINGTON TO MT MARTHA CLIFFTOP WALK

This must-do easy trek, is one of the best clifftop walks on the peninsula as there are continually changing views with many lookout points and you can even use the occasional seat to rest and take in the panorama.

Start	Linley Point opposite King Georges Avenue, Mornington
Distance	5 kilometres one way
Time	Up to 1.5 hours
Effort	Easy to medium
Maps	Melways Map 145 B1 Linley Point
When	Anytime

Walk out to Linley Point. Notice a picnic rotunda and taking in a number of viewing platforms that look north, south and approximately due west. Collectively, there are great panoramic views of the Mornington coastline and Port Phillip Bay. From the southern lookout at Linley Point you will be able to discern Mt.Martha Beach and the associated boat sheds, which is your objective some 5 kilometres away. A memorial commemorates the exploits of the Lady Nelson in 1802 under the command of Lieut. John Murray.

Opposite Strachans Road the gravel track is very close to the road. Don't be disappointed as the track soon winds its way closer to the clifftops with sufficient vegetation between you and the road to obscure a lot of the vehicular traffic. This clifftop walk is reasonably sheltered

Mornington to Mt Martha Clifftop Walk.

from winds as well as sun until the beach section of the walk at Mount Martha is encountered.

There is another lookout with views back towards Linley Point with the You Yangs to the west, Port Phillip heads the southwest and the CBD skyline. The nearby lookout will also give you views toward Arthurs Seat.

Recently installed signage by the Mornington Peninsula Shire indicates dogs must be on a lead and cyclists are prohibited. This makes for a safer pedestrian route which has always been very popular when I have walked in this area. Families with strollers, runners and joggers, as well as power walkers all make use of this very user-friendly track which is well gravelled and well maintained with scarcely one puddle even during the winter months. If you intend walking down to any of these small beaches along the cliffs, I would strongly recommend Birdrock Beach as the place to see. With a delightful offshore reef and a protected beach with small headlands at either end, this is one of the most picturesque locations in the area. A great place for a swim on a summer's day or simply sit on the beach with a picnic in cooler weather and experience the grandeur of nature.

Fit walkers and those on an exercise regime may find themselves walking up to 7 kilometres an hour with the likely outcome of arriving at Mount Martha beach well within the hour. There are access points to Fossil Beach and Dava Beach opposite the Dava hotel where there is also a lookout. It is worthwhile to take the side tracks to every lookout to gain great views along this walk. These side tracks to the lookouts are usually less than 50 metres from the main track. Some of the better lookout points have timber decks and seats as well as fencing. Approaching the track opposite Craigie Road the walking track runs very close to the Esplanade within 500 metres of Craigie Rd. Half a kilometre south of Craigie Road there is a fire access path that runs down to Mount Martha Beach North. Take this access road to the beach. You will see the You Yangs in the distance, which are over 50 kilometres away.

Continue walking on the beach, now at a considerably slower pace on the sand, past the very brightly coloured boat sheds. This part of the walk is in great contrast to the clifftop walk which passes through coastal scrub. You are heading towards Mount Martha Village. As you walk into civilisation a carpark comes into view. An old but delightfully painted amenities block with picnic tables nearby may also be a good place for a break. Shortly you will pass the Mount Martha Lifesaving Club. These clubs are always a hive of activity during the summer months. Walkers may wish to add a little extra time and make a cafe or lunch stop at the delightful Mount Martha Village. This will add another 500 metres to the walk. Return via the same route to the start of your walk.

This area has the potential for a great long-distance walk which would be the extension of the Mornington to Mount Martha walk. Imagine a spectacular walk from Balcombe Point all the way to Martha Point and on to Safety Beach, and Dromana. Wow!

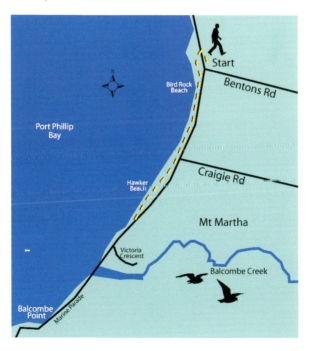

MT MARTHA COMMUNITY FOREST

A simple circuit walk through open forest, this will test your fitness with a steady climb from the creek which forms part of the eastern section of this loop. The leash-free status may be the perfect place to indulge your pooch.

Start	Nepean Highway, opposite Balcombe Grammar School
Distance	3 kilometres
Time	Under 45 minutes
Grade	Easy to medium
Maps	Melways map 151 C2
When	Anytime
Note	This is a leash-free area for dogs

Start this easy walk by passing through the gate and heading to your left or due north. The wide track makes for easy walking and the surrounding trees, mainly eucalypts and she-oaks, provide shelter from wind and sun. This section of the track is flat and has been revegetated in recent years. After walking about 500 metres the path heads down the hill, due east and towards the small creek and gully. The downhill section is considerably shorter and before long you will change direction again. After walking on a southerly bearing for another half a kilometre the uphill workout begins. Take a slow and steady pace to arrive back at the start of this walk.

This could be a great walk and venue for a workout to test your fitness

Mt Martha Community Forest.

level. Timing yourself over the distance as well as checking your speed with a GPS can be fun as well as setting a challenge for the next 'time-trial' after a training program. Don't forget to log your details for comparison on the next trial.

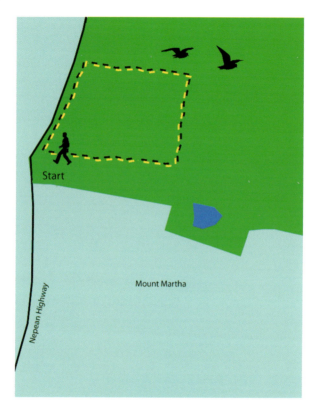

MT MARTHA PARK

This relaxed walking trail with delightful, sheltered picnic grounds, passes the summit of Mt Martha. There are a number of possible loop circuits to choose from. Information on the area is available at the start of the walk.

Start	Forest Drive and Park Road, Mt Martha
Distance	2+ kilometres
Time	Less than 1 hour
Effort	Easy to medium
Maps	Melways 150 H7
When	Anytime except Code Red days

Prior to the commencement of your walk peruse the detailed information boards nearby. These highlight the flora and fauna of the area. (Note: Some of the information is out of date as there were pictures from the lookout tower which is no longer in use.) There are snow gums, coastal mana gums and phosphorescent fungus which is known to glow green at night. Koalas possums, lizards, echidnas and wallabies have also been observed in this park.

The Boonerwurrung aboriginal community was one of six aboriginal clans who inhabited the area. Information displayed also details the walking tracks in the park.

Grimwood Nature Walk takes you though black sheoak groves near the former lookout tower.

The Calder Nature Walk takes you through snow gums and grassy

Mt Martha Park.

woodlands via the summit. This track is well maintained and suitable for strollers, I noticed a family with two young children taking advantage of a sunny autumn afternoon.

I started this exploratory walk by walking through the main gate and bearing left at any of the 'decision points' aiming for the derelict lookout tower.

On the way you will pass the summit, marked with a pole which indicates an elevation of 166 metres however the GPS indicated only 155 metres. There is no view at the summit. To get to the lookout area continue on this track, walk through another open gateway on your left and turn right, following the signed marker post to the lookout. As of early 2011, the lookout is closed. There is no stairway available and signage indicates the structure is condemned. Hopefully in the near future, a new lookout tower will be built or perhaps the ground could be cleared to seaward to allow for views towards Arthurs Seat and Port Phillip Heads through to the You Yangs and beyond.

Your Melways map indicates a spider web of walking paths and management vehicle access tracks. While this may seem confusing, it is difficult to get lost here as the park is surrounded on all sides by roads. The main aim is to keep up higher near the summit area and walk in a loop that will get you comfortably back to your starting point.

I chose to follow the Grimwood nature trail on the return journey which is relatively well signposted. The children's playground equipment at the Mt Martha Park was being utilised by a group of families and their children celebrating a birthday witnessed by their small marquee with lots of balloons and guest magicians who were also taking part in the festivities.

As on my previous visit to this park, an injection of funds would help to smarten up this unique part of the peninsula. The reinstatement of the lookout tower would give walkers a definite objective as well as the photographic high point for the walk.

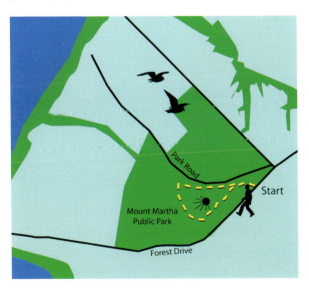

NUMBER 16 TO KOONYA OCEAN BEACH

An ocean breeze, surf breaking on the shore, gannets skimming the ocean swell, container ships at sea, rugged coastal scenery, sheltered inland paths and exposed tracks open to ever-restless Bass Strait. Come and experience it all.

Start	No 16 Carpark opposite Marcia Ave, Rye
Distance	4.5 km one way
Time	Allow at least 2 hours
Grade	Medium
Maps	Melways Map 167 J10
When	Anytime
Note	You are advised not to swim at any unpatrolled ocean beaches

There is limited car parking at Number 16 carpark. Take the track that heads out towards the lookout, clearly marked on your Melways Map. This vantage point gives commanding views of the immediate coastline and towards Cape Schanck, to the southeast. Now take the walking track to Bridgewater Bay which starts 50 metres along the gravel roadway on your right. The track has a boom gate and an orange direction marker. You are now heading in a north westerly direction. During spring there are many wildflowers including the bearded heath, ti tree, dolichos, native daisies and pig face. The walking path, wide and reasonably flat, now parallels Tasman Drive. Bird life can be heard along this path and there are a number of side tracks which are indicated in your Melways Map, which will take you to vantage points within the National Park.

Number 16 to Koonya Ocean Beach.

The track is sheltered from onshore winds, and trees would give partial shade during the warmer days of the year. As you approach a parking area off Tasman Drive there is a delightful stand of Moonah trees. These trees can grow for many hundreds of years and they are protected throughout the Mornington Peninsula. Every few hundred metres or at a track junction there are marker posts with orange arrows and a walkers logo will be visible. These will keep you headed in the right direction. It is very hard to get lost here and the track had been recently maintained on my last walk through the area.

Signage at the entrance to Dimmicks Beach indicates that a local volunteer group is involved in the care and upkeep of this beautiful area. When you arrive at a T intersection, take the left hand signposted track. The right hand track taking you back to the car park. Now take the track to Dimmicks Beach which is only signposted from the car park. Walkers may miss this signage as you continue along the walking track. This is where your copy of a map comes in very handy. The track out to Dimmicks Beach becomes sandy and ocean views are the order of the day. Take note of the advisory signage indicating dangerous surf, currents and unstable cliffs. This signage is surrounded by shell debris: The site of aboriginal middens. As these sites are of historical and cultural significance, items must not be disturbed but do look for different coloured rocks amongst the pale sands and sun bleached shells. These rocks may well be scrapers and implements used by the former inhabitants of the area.

As you approach the beach a well-placed timber seat comes into view. This may well be a viewpoint and a place to engage your camera. In November a number of seabirds, shearwaters, were observed to be washed up on the beach, having travelled thousands of kilometres. It is probably not surprising to see some of the birds meet their demise. These incredible birds fly over 8000 kilometres to the Aleutian Islands and Alaska!

From Dimmicks Beach the walking track skirts the coastline, affording great views towards the Bellarine Peninsula. Pearce's Beach is the next small cove along this rocky coastline and the distinctive Bridgwater Bay will shortly come into view. The bridge is at the southern end of the beach, and stairway access is gained from the middle part of this cove. This is another good place to investigate the shoreline. However when I last visited this area in mid-spring 2010, the tide was very high, the surf being around 1.5 metres and much of the beach was inundated. In situations such as these I advise keeping off the beach, particularly if the waves are surging high up onto the sandy the shoreline.

The track continues towards the next small headland at the north western end of Bridgewater Bay, Koreen Point. Here you should take the right hand fork which meets up with the inland track taking you back to the St Johns Wood Road car park. Just before the car park the so-called 'Life-Saving Track' will speed you on your way towards Sorrento. From here you are around 2 kilometres from your destination,

Koonya Ocean Beach. This track winds through the coastal bush, although slower progress can be made skirting the dunes and clifftops around the coast. Caution does need to be exercised if this is your preferred option as there are precipitous drop-offs and unstable cliffs. It is more prudent and better for the fragile coastal ecosystem to take the inland path.

Take the time to gaze out to sea along this part of the coastline. Spectacular cold fronts with their associated cloud masses can often be seen ushering in from Bass Strait and the Southern Ocean. Majestic clouds and deep blue skies can add to an already splendid vista. Nature is at its best here. Far from Melbourne's urbanization of roads and houses and all the trappings of city life, here we have the untamed and powerful sea, jagged rocks and cliffs, blustery winds and vegetation that hangs on for dear life as the wind moves the very earth and sand on which this vegetation depends. Arriving at Koonya Ocean Beach the decision is to phone your chauffeur or start the return journey. Happy walking.

Note: Walkers could commence their journey at any of the carparks and roads that abut the national park here. Adjust your walking times and distances accordingly.

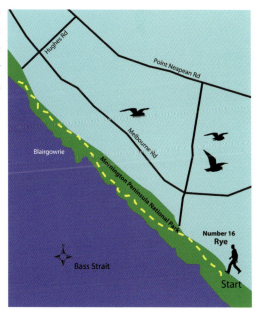

NUMBER 16 TO RYE OCEAN BEACH

Rugged, sandy ocean beaches, clifftop views, shorebirds gliding along the ocean waves and entrancing rock pools. They are all here and more. Surfers, divers, fishing boats and container ships as well as the occasional yacht also add interest to this iconic park. The Mornington Peninsula National Park stretches for 30 kilometres and this section of coast is amongst the best.

Start	Number 16 carpark, Browns Road, Rye
Distance	7 kilometres return
Time	2+ hour return.
Effort	Medium
Maps	Melways map 167 J10
When	Low tides and low swell preferred

Leaving the carpark, head out for the track that heads towards the lookout, clearly marked on your Melways Map. This vantage point gives great views of the coastline towards Cape Schanck to the southeast. Now head out for the beach and the first feature 'lizard rock', a sandstone rock which is close to the shoreline on high tide.

Continue along the beach towards Orr Point, a small elevated headland which can be walked around at low tides only. Be careful to keep well back from the shoreline if surf is breaking and surging up onto the beach. As you approach Orr Point there are some walking track markers which will guide you over the top of this headland. Some great views of the coast towards Gunnamatta and Cape Schanck are possible on

Beached Mini Blue Whale, Rye Ocean Beach.

clear days. Also observe evidence of extensive shell middens in this area. If you venture around the point on low tide you cannot fail to be impressed by the rock pools and bubble weed which clings tenaciously to the shallow sea floor here. There is a very popular surfing break called 'snatches' on the Rye Ocean Beach side of Orr Point. The track, flanked with low coastal scrub, meanders its way along the top of the cliffs and slowly descends towards the beach over a distance of about 300 metres. As the track starts to deteriorate and your elevation gets lower you will be able to find an easy access point to the beach below.

This section of coast, particularly between Orr Point and Rye Ocean Beach can harbour some interesting items washed up on the high tide line. The author has founded a migratory bird on this beach which had been banded one month earlier in New Zealand. The whale pictured was an adult female pygmy blue whale, 22 metres in length.

Shearwater Rye Ocean Beach.

This stranding occurred in 2009. Apart from pieces of driftwood and fishing gear which also gets washed up on this part of the coast, pumice stone, a volcanic rock that floats on water, can also be found from time to time. The pumice comes from volcanic areas far to the north of Australia and floats down the east coast of Australia on the Eastern Australian Current.

Continue along the coast, again looking out to sea continuously to check on wave height and behaviour. You will already have checked your tide guide. With an incoming tide and offshore wind, swell can be two or more metres in height and often over three or four metres. These waves can surge high up onto the beach for many metres. You are advised to walk well back from the waters edge and ensure that all the walkers in your group are aware of the dangers along this coastline.

The water can be two or three metres deep very close to the shore and this coastline is prone to rips and currents.

You will approach another two small headlands. Tide and sea conditions will dictate whether you walk along the beach and rocks or go up and around the headlands on rough 'walking tracks' which walkers, surfers and beach goers have used over the years. Rye Ocean Beach should be easily discernable with its stairway access points and usually any number of vehicles which are parked to gain views of the coastline. Fisherman, beach goers and surfers all make the most of this very popular ocean beach. Return via the same way or use your second vehicle. Perhaps you can phone for your chauffeur to pick you up?

Number 16 Beach is an unusual name which is derived from the fact that this beach is the 16th beach or 'gap' from Point Nepean or 'the Heads' as it is known by locals.

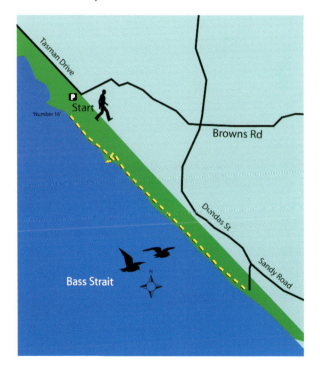

OT DAM AND ARTHURS SEAT STATE PARK

The impressive OT Dam is a jewel on the peninsula. This picturesque lake will surprise you with its charm. This is 'tranquillity base'. A short walk on well-maintained tracks, this walk is within everyones' capability.

Start	OT Track, Arthurs Seat Road, 400 metres west of Main Creek Road
Distance	2 kilometres return
Time	Under 1 hour
Effort	Easy to medium
Maps	Melways map 171 K2
When	Anytime except Code Red days

The signposted path is actually a management vehicle track which heads out towards the OT Dam 1 kilometre away. At the first intersection take the left hand track where a sign indicates the OT Dam is 500 metres. The right hand four-wheel-drive track descends towards the OT Dam as well and you can use this for the return journey. You will pass the Friends Track (see walk number 3) which is on your left.

On your left and beyond barrier fencing is the impressive Hillview Quarry. Look for any small access paths which terminate at this fence and afford great views of this operational quarry. This quarry has donated millions of dollars to the local community over the years and its unusual brown granite is sort after from interstate customers.

The track to the dam is easily followed, being well signposted and

OT Dam.

within a quarter of a kilometre you will have arrived at your destination. Approach this dam quietly and you may be rewarded with the sight of birds and animals using this former water supply.

There is a spillway here as well as some good vantage points for a 'photographic' opportunity. Take time to investigate the shoreline of this very picturesque dam, a former campsite and water supply for a jam making industry many years ago.

While there is little in the way of picnic facilities here, the dam is still a great location for a picnic or snack break. Our family have had many lunch and 'tea' breaks using a small light-weight stove to 'boil the billy', particularly on a cool winters' day. Hot chocolate anyone?

Return via the path which picks up the wide fire access track which heads southwest from this channel and spillway. This track is shown on the Parks Victoria publication: Arthurs Seat State Park and Summit. See www.parkweb.vic.gov.au/resources05/05_0457.pdf

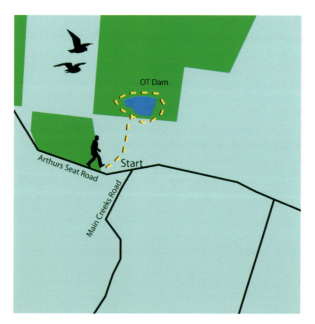

PENINSULA GARDENS BUSHLAND RESERVE, ROSEBUD

A reserve of substantial area with a rehabilitation program well underway will see this readily accessible part of the peninsula become more popular in time. This reserve is also one of the last remaining areas of indigenous remnant bush left existing on the Mornington Peninsula.

Start	Jetty Road, Rosebud South
Distance	2.5 kilometres
Time	Under 1 hour
Grade	Undulating, some sandy patches
Map	Melways Map 170 H10
When	Anytime. Avoid total fire ban days.
Website	www.peninsulagardens.org

Access to this reserve is about half a kilometre south of the entrance to Peninsula Sands housing estate. Parking for vehicles has yet to be developed here and the entrance gate allows access for walkers only. The gravel management vehicle track heads in a north-easterly direction, passing an interesting stand of native vegetation.

The main vegetation here is eucalypt woodland with a dry heath understorey. Bracken, eucalypts, ti-tree, acacia and grass trees form the main vegetative species here. Near the entrance there is a thick forest of lilly-pilly on your right which is rather unusual in this area. The track is sandy in parts and reminds me of parts of the Langwarrin Reserve

Peninsula flora.

Grass tree, Peninsula Gardens Bushlands Reserve.

at Baxter. As you slowly ascend a low hill many grass trees will come into view on your right. Take the left fork in the track which heads out towards a grassed area adjacent to Drum Drum Alloc Creek.

Tiger snakes are known to inhabit this location and in warmer months they will be active. (Have you taken your first aid kit?) Inspect the water course before returning back along the same route but this time taking the sandy left hand track which passes impressive stands of meleleuca, she-oaks, eucalypts and numerous grass trees over two metres in height, some with very prominent spears. Follow this track towards the Jetty Road boundary. As you approach the main road take the right hand track. (The left hand or east track will lead you directly into a farming property.) Shortly you will pass by a damp and darker forested area with kangaroo paw ferns. The track meanders roughly north before changing direction again and eventually linking up with the main 4WD track which you can use to return to the starting point at the Jetty Road entrance. Look out for birds such as the crimson rosellas and nches.

At the time of writing, walker access via the Drum Drum Alloc Creek gate was not available. In any case this recently re-vegetated area is not overly appealing nor is the pathway adjacent to the housing estate. A far better option is to be surrounded on all sides by the native bushland, using the main entrance access point. Cinnamon fungus is also a problem within the reserve, especially as grass-trees are susceptible. In time, footwear-cleaning facilities may also be introduced.

A 'Friends of the Peninsula Gardens Bushland Reserve' can be accessed via the website: http://www.peninsulagardens.org/about-us.html

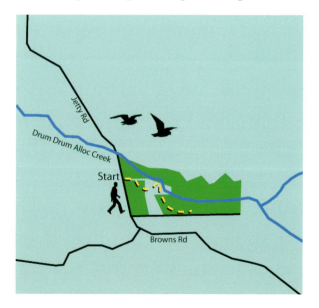

POINT LEO

The delightful Point Leo is one of my all-time favourites on the peninsula having camped and surfed here from my teenage days. This peaceful and scenic location is a buzz of activity over the summer camping season. Contrast this with the cold winter season when wind and rain squalls have 'cleared the beaches' of human habitation. There are lots of options here. Walking on the beach and the foreshore, camping grounds and a boardwalk as well as the lookouts.

Start	Point Leo foreshore, Point Leo Road
Distance	2 to 4 kilometres return
Time	Up to 1 hour
Effort	Easy
Maps	Melways map 257 C5
When	Anytime low tide preferable

Park your vehicle at any convenient beach access point near the 'gatehouse' and shops at the entrance to Point Leo. Walk out onto the beach and aim for the headland, walking past Point Leo Boat Club on low tides. Return via the Surf Club access point and walk back to your vehicle via the road. At high tides the beach walk past the boat club may be impassable and you may need to head up onto the headland and walking track which skirts the foreshore and passes to the rear of this boat club. There is an excellent but short boardwalk from near the entry gate to the start of the gravel walking track that winds around the headland, past the boat club and up to the top carpark. Near the boat club you will find barbecues, shelter, tables and a children's playground.

Point Leo.

With solid summer and autumn rain and the sun shining on an early Sunday morning, and with no surf to attract the many surfers who frequent this area, Point Leo was very peaceful, intensely green and simply a magnificent location!

On both sides of Point Leo Boat Club there are substantial wooden stairways which lead to the walking track and roadway. Both the track and roadway take you to another lookout which faces due east and another stairway descends towards the beach at the bottom of the headland.

At the end of the easterly facing car park on the top of the headland are picnic tables. A plaque here commemorates the establishment of artillery used to guard the entrance to Western Port Bay during the Second World War. A direction rose indicates Launceston is 390 kilometres southeast.

The camping area surrounding the headland and back towards the surf club would be a hive of activity between Melbourne Cup Day weekend and Easter.

Substantial erosion has occurred on the sand dunes to the west of the headland, on the exposed ocean side of the point. Erosion of up to 3 metres indicates that heavy swell can damage the fragile coastal dune systems here.

At low tide there is an expansive sandy beach in front of the iconic Point Leo Surf Lifesaving Club. Notice the distinctive watchtower of the surf club which was in winter recess when I last walked here. It is comforting to know that lifesaving clubs have been protecting our shores and swimmers for well over one hundred years. Please support your local surf club.

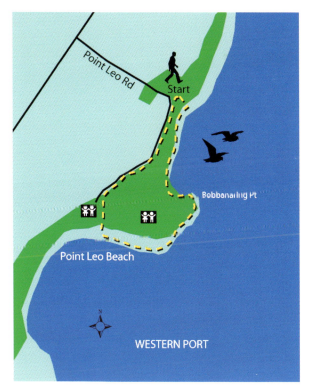

POINT LEO TO
BALNARRING BEACH

A highly recommended walk which allows you to experience a wildcoast environment. Remnant coastal vegetation and firm sand on a relatively flat beach all make for enjoyable and easy walking.

Start	End of Point Leo Road, near East Creek
Distance	11 kilometres return
Time	3 hours
Effort	Easy to medium. Flat beach walking
Maps	Melways map 257 C5
When	Anytime, low tides preferable

Park your vehicle at the beach car park, below the gate house on Point Leo Road. The walk commences from the carpark just above the beach park and crosses East Creek, which may necessitate the removal of your footwear.

I set out at around 9 am on a Sunday morning with a 0.18 metre low tide giving plenty of firm sand for good traction and a reasonable walking speed. The beach is ideal for baby strollers and a few families were putting in some kilometres between Point Leo and Merricks Beach.

Approximately 1 kilometre towards Balnarring there is a heavily eroded section of foredune about one metre in height. At very high tides this section of coast would become impassable and is best left for more suitable conditions. There is much bird life in evidence and the blooms

Point Leo to Balnarring Beach.

of the banksia trees were offering plenty of feed. This section of coast has very few dwellings to be seen. The farm houses are set well back from the beach and a sense of desolation and a wilderness permeates the walker.

Coming within a kilometre of the Merricks Yacht Club you will notice the stepped vegetation from low fore dunes through to medium and then higher trees abutting the residential homes and farmland. There is a walkway and entry point near the yacht club. Nearby is a creek with a stagnant pool of water which, in wetter times, would probably flow out to sea. At this point in time there was a lot of timber and flotsam washed into the creek, similar to the backwaters of Rutledge Creek in the Port Campbell National Park.

Heading past the club you will see a point or headland beyond. There is a delightfully small cove and the sweeping arc of the beach gives a personal feel to this particular area of coast. On the low tides notice some relatively high ridges of basalt rock, somewhat similar to the rock formations between Bear Gully and Cape Liptrap in South Gippsland. Again, there is substantial evidence of erosion on this section of coast and any keen walkers attempting this hike on higher tide levels would have to walk up on the foredune to make any headway. There is another small headland to negotiate before reaching Balnarring Beach. The options are to walk around the small point over the rocks, placed here for erosion control, or to walk up the steps and onto a path which passes through a bird sanctuary. A revegetation program has been very successful here. Within 300 metres you will have arrived at Balnarring Beach Road ready for you vehicular pickup or simply return the way you came.

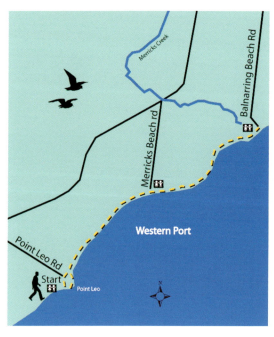

POINT NEPEAN NATIONAL PARK

History and rugged ocean coastline, walking tracks and manicured lawns, defence fortifications and serene grandeur: Point Nepean National Park offers all this and more. Being one of the more accessible and larger parks on the peninsula, this is an area which must be seen and revisited such is the extent of the attractions on offer here.

Start	Point Nepean Park Entrance, end of Point Nepean Rd, Portsea.
Distance	2 to 15+ kilometres
Time	Minimum 2 hours. Allow 5+ hours if possible.
Grade	Easy to medium
Maps	Melways Map 156 C2, Point Nepean National Park, Visitor Guide Parknotes June 2010.
When	Anytime subject to weather conditions. The Park is open 24 hours. Admission fees were abolished in 2010.
Note	The gates for vehicle access to Gunners Cottage are open from 8-00am to 5-00pm. The Transporter operates from 10-00am to 5-00pm. On Code Red Fire Danger days the park will be closed for public safety
Suggestion	Take binoculars

Please visit the Information Centre at the park entrance. Apart from booking the transporter there is an excellent, detailed relief map of the National Park which indicates the time frames necessary to investigate

Bay and Ocean, Point Nepean National Park.

the Park. These range from one hour, through two and four hours to an all-day investigation. Pamphlets available at the Information Centre as well as there is video presentation available in the theatrette.

This is a large park and walking can be as challenging as you like. It is over six kilometres from the park entrance to the tip at Point Nepean. There are some small hills that offer a solid, if short workout for keen walkers between the park entrance and Point Nepean. This area offers so many choices that the initial problem is where to start. I suggest to follow a sequence from the entrance and Information Centre at the start of the park.

There are 5 main areas to focus your walks:

1. Police Point

2. Quarantine Station

3. Observatory Point

4. Cheviot Hill

5. Point Nepean

Options may include: Visiting the majority of sites in one day or making several visits over a period of time to maximize your time and exploration of this outstanding National Park. I would also suggest using the transporter for part of the return journey. The transporter also has a rolling audio presentation which gives interesting details about the national park en route. This may be particularly suitable for first-time visitors to the park.

1. POLICE POINT BUSHLAND RESERVE

20 minutes less than 1 km

Don't miss this hidden part of Portsea. Immediately inside the front entrance is a side road on your right which passes some weatherboard houses. Walk past these dwellings and onto sprawling lawns. At the high viewpoint to the east is a great view of Weeroona Bay and Portsea Jetty. Nearby is one of the artist trail signs, a painting by Penleigh Boyd, depicting the Portsea Jetty in 1921.

This almost forgotten part of the park is a delightful area. These well maintained weatherboard homes formed part of the Defence Force's accommodation for personnel. When my partner and I first visited the 'base' many years ago there was an immediate 'atmosphere' or feel here that reminded us of the tranquillity of French Island and Flinders Island. There is no hustle and bustle. Here is a by-gone era where time moved at a more sedate pace. Time to listen to the wind in the trees and watch the grass grow!

Quarantine station.

2. QUARANTINE STATION AND THE COLES TRACK

Quarantine Station to Gunners Cottage approx 1.6 kilometres and 20 minutes easy walking

Walk along Defence Road for about 1 kilometre until Ochiltree Road and the entrance to the Quarantine Station. Within 500 metres you will arrive at the imposing establishment that was initially a Quaratine Station and more latterly offices and training quarters for Defence Force personnel.

This is a great site to investigate. Sprawling lawns, historic buildings, great views of the bay and Queenscliff to the northwest all make for a special experience in the largest 'park' on the Peninsula. The Quarantine Station, established in 1852, is an interesting area to explore. The giant autoclave and the exhibits on display in the buildings here offer a great insight into life many years ago.

Note: There is an excellent brochure entitled: **The Point Nepean Quarantine Station: A Self Guided Tour** which details the main historic buildings and their associated history which may be available at the entrance to the park as well as Visitor Information Centres.

At the time of going to print, there appears to be interest in building a jetty to access this part of the park. Beach access is also being established.

The following address:
http://www.parkweb.vic.gov.au/4pn-oralhistory.cfm

...contains video interviews with a number of people who have been associated with the Quarantine Station.

Those wishing to extend this walk can pick up the Coles Track which continues all the way to the Cheviot Hill stop. This is a fairly sheltered walk with occasional glimpses of the bay. This gravel track has been recently constructed and is also suitable for strollers and bicycles.

It is approximately 2.5 kilometres from the Quarantine Station to Cheviot Hill stop and around 30 minutes walking time

3. OBSERVATORY POINT CEMETERY WALTER PISTERMAN WALK

800 metres and 30 minutes

Observatory Point from Gunners Cottage is about 800 metres return from the cottage, due north, and towards the bay. A number of sheltered picnic tables are located here and there is access to the remains of the cattle jetty and a picturesque sandy beach. Please note: Swimming is not advised along any of the bayside beaches in the park due to very strong tides. If time allows visit the nearby cemetery, which is clearly

Cheviot Hill fortifications.

signposted from the Gunners Cottage. Those keen on a sandy beach walk can gain access to the 'Bay Beach Walk' from Observatory Point, The Bend and near the Jarman Oval. The beach walk is about 2.5 kilometres in length.

4. CHEVIOT HILL

600 metres 25 minutes

Gun emplacements, the death of a Prime Minister and a shipwreck all contribute to an impressive, short, interesting walk of less than a kilometre. This walk has it all, being well within the capabilities of all ages of walkers, everyone will find something of interest here. A must-do walk.

This very rewarding walk on a gravel and asphalt path with some steps, will stimulate the senses and maximize the thrill while minimizing the sweat required to make the 'summit' of Cheviot Hill. At 54 metres there are commanding views of The Rip, Bass Strait, and the Surf Coast towards Cape Otway. The Bluff at Barwon Heads should be easily discernable on most days. Looking east Arthurs Seat and Mt Martha are visible and to the southeast Cape Schanck is visible at 30 kilometres on clear days with good visibililty.

This area takes its name from 'The Cheviot', a ship which foundered here 1887. The Cheviot ran aground on a nearby reef with the loss of 35 lives. It is noteworthy that there are more than a dozen shipwrecks in the immediate vicinity of Point Nepean such is the treacherousness of the waters in this area.

Point Nepean National Park.

In 1967 the then Prime Minister, Harold Holt, disappeared while swimming at this ocean beach. As well, a large shield, used to protect gunners, resembles a massive warriors' helmet from ancient Greece. The 'battle armour' is a standout feature here. As well, there are great views of this very expansive area. An alternative return journey to Cheviot Hill stop may be made via the Happy Valley Walk. Add another 700 metres and 20 minutes.

Walkers wanting further challenges may decide to take the Rifle Range Walk, a recently constructed loop walk, to vary your return to Gunners Cottage. Take the newer track which skirts the fence line. While less interesting, there is shelter from the wind, if required, and it is a different return route to the Gunners Cottage.

5. FORT NEPEAN AND POINT NEPEAN

Allow 1 hour. Distance up to 1 kilometre. Some optional steep steps.

Fort Nepean is an exciting place for adults and children alike. There is a real history here. Gun emplacements, an engine house, tunnels and lookouts are ready to touch, feel and see. The fortress Point Nepean rests on a slither of land dividing Bass Strait from Port Philip Bay. The location is dramatic. Surf is usually pounding on the ocean beaches while the quieter bay area adds an air of calmness to the scene before you. The only shelter here for walkers is provided by the tunnels and other associated infrastructure. It's best to get a forecast before exploring Point Nepean as the coastline can receive the full force of south-westerly gales from Bass Strait and the Southern Ocean.

There are interesting times ahead for Point Nepean National Park with proposals to offer a range of accommodation within the park as well as the reinstatement of a jetty.

The following address:
http://www.parkweb.vic.gov.au/1podcasts_Point_Nepean.cfm

...has four self-guided walks and five audio guides on the history of the area. These self-guided walks can be downloaded to your MP3 player or iPod.

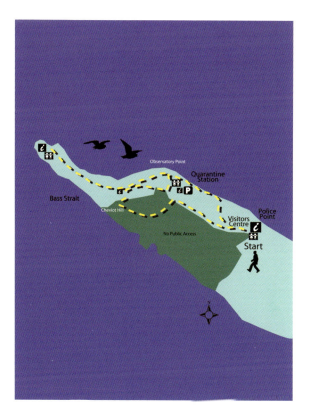

PORTSEA OCEAN BEACH TO LONDON BRIDGE

I love the ocean and I love all things 'oceanic'. I love a wide sandy beach and the salt spray generated by ocean waves and wind. So this walk has it all for me. A quick escape, a short walk but big on impact. Great views from the Farnsworth Track. Do it all in an hour.

Start	Capark adjacent to Portsea Surf Life Saving Club
Distance	Up to 3 kilometres, circuit
Time	1 hour 20 mins
Effort	Easy to medium, steps
Maps	Melways map156 C6
When	Anytime. Lower tides make for easier beach walking

Parking is available at the lower car park near Portsea Surf Life Club. Take the paved stairway down to the beach, passing signage indicating this beach is a habitat for protected shore birds.

Walking on an expansive area of sandy beach at low tide and with only three other people on this beach, the three hooded plover that were feeding above the low tide line were looking for anything the ocean had washed onto the shoreline. These endangered shorebirds seemed brave as they did not fly off when I walked closer to take a photograph.

About, a hundred metres west of the surf club there is evidence of extensive erosion on the sand dunes. With a very high tide this beach would be almost impassable. I estimated the wind strength, from

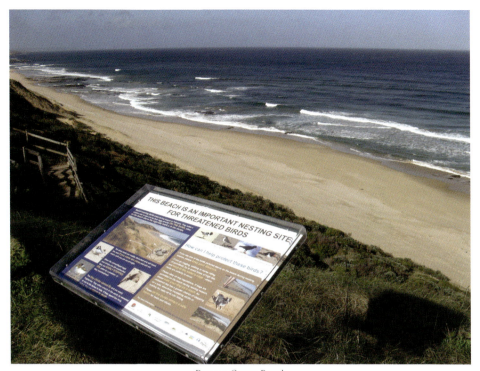

Portsea Ocean Beach.

the southeast, at 15 kilometres per hour but looking at the weather observations later in the day the wind strength at South Channel Fort was nearly twice this speed.

Looking skywards I noticed a small plane inbound for Melbourne from Bass Strait. This was a King Island Airlines twin-engine aircraft cruising at around 3000 - 4000 feet. This was an unusual track for this plane, being far to the west of its normal flight path. With strong easterly winds and low pressure trough in Eastern Bass Strait that brought a hundred millimetres of rain to Gippsland and some local flooding.

Halfway along the beach between the surf club and London Bridge there was an area that had been extensively gouged out by the sea. This area had a high embankment or 'cliff' of well over a metre and it could be dangerous to walk below this area with an incoming tide as

London Bridge, Portsea.

surging waves can quickly inundate the foreshore as they get funnelled and their speed seems to increase as they break on the shore. Again take extreme care on surf beaches, particularly if you are unfamiliar with sea conditions. I like to think my experience surfing, diving and boating as well as a coast guard navigation course and surf lifesaving training have combined to give me a healthy respect for and some understanding of the sea and its behaviour.

This is a great beach walk, absolutely 'oceanic' in experience. Wide sands give a real sense of freedom. The low tide exposes extensive rock platforms and there are patches of bull kelp to be seen. This large seaweed is unusual along this part of the coastline, it is more likely to be seen in vast quantities on the west coast of King island. (See 'Walks of King Island by K. Martin.) With the sun shining, a blue sky above and a bracing wind, all combined to make for a really enjoyable walk.

As you approach London Bridge notice a curved walking ramp which takes you back to the top car park. You will pick this up on your return journey.

Within 200 metres of London Bridge the coastal geography changes from low scrub clinging to the high sand dunes. Now there are bare sandstone cliffs which have no vegetation at all on the more vertical faces and it is easy to see the layering of this sedimentary rock. Very close to London Bridge is an extensive rock pool visible on the low tide. On my walk here a large volume of bubble weed (seaweed) had washed up on the shoreline.

At London Bridge there are interesting rock stacks and formations. Beyond the 'bridge' is another headland with a dilapidated cyclone fence. This marks the start of the Point Nepean National Park and the former defence force base. This area is off limits due to unexploded ordnance. It would be fantastic to see this beach cleared of unexploded munitions so that walkers could walk along the coast to Point Nepean.

A reminder to please avoid sandstone cliffs and caves. Nine people perished at Margaret River, Western Australia, while sheltering under a cliff some years ago.

Two Sooty Oyster Catchers were observed very close to the water's edge. These birds are identified by their black bodies and distinctive slender and long, orange beaks.

After investigating London Bridge head back to Portsea Ocean Beach via the Farnsworth Walking Track which is about 1.5 kilometres in length. You need to walk up the ramp to the main car park. This is a good workout even though you'll be at the top of the ramp within 5 minutes. Walk towards the amenities block. The start of the Farnsworth Walking Track is adjacent to the amenities block. New signage details information on London Bridge and Point Nepean National Park, as well as a detailed map of the walking tracks here.

The inland track is gravelled and sheltered from the wind and sun as it winds its way through a small gully. Part of this track surface has been asphalted. However, later it turns to sand, and is still very serviceable as a good walking track. The first lookout gives commanding views towards Cape Schanck, 30 kilometres away and there are also good views towards Point Nepean. The Bluff at Barwon Heads and Ocean Grove are also visible. Notice the meanderings of the Farnsworth track as it winds its way through the coastal scrub to Portsea Ocean Beach car park.

Further along the track a high point gives views towards Portsea Golf Club and Port Phillip Bay. Take advantage of the seat here to take in this view. Moving closer to Portsea Ocean Beach the track follows a ridge and it is more exposed to wind and the elements. A second lookout gives views towards Arthurs Seat and Mud Island. Descend a flight of stairs out to the car park. Head diagonally across this carpark towards a pedestrian crossing and amenities block. Pick up the walking track again which runs behind the Portsea Surf Club. Signage indicates the flora and fauna of the area, some history and a very detailed map. I hope you enjoyed your walk.

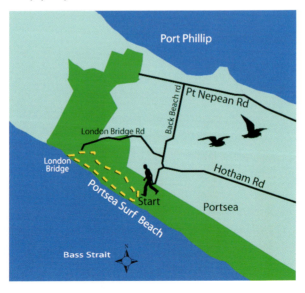

PORTSEA TO SORRENTO ARTISTS TRAIL

Try something completely different. Take a grand tour past the ritzy Portsea waterfront properties and experience the views as seen by many of our famous artists.

Start	Police Point, Point Nepean National Park, Portsea
Distance	Around 6 kilometres one way
Time	Allow up to 2 hours ramble and amble, with a café stop at Portsea or Sorrento
Effort	Easy to medium
Maps	Melways 156 C2,
When	Anytime
Suggestion	Complete this walk over the warmer months of the year when scores of pleasure craft are moored along the very scenic coastline. Possible return from Sorrento on the bus 788.

Start at Point Nepean National Park, parking your vehicle near the information Centre, amenities block and barbecues.

Walk back towards the main entrance and follow the road past a series of houses on your right. Path signage will soon indicate that you are heading towards Police Point, approximately 7 minutes walk from the information centre. As you walk into Police Point notice the circular concrete dome near the last house. This appears to have been a well and the associated footings may well have been for a windmill in the early days of settlement. Follow the path past this house and towards Portsea Pier, due east.

The first painting depicted is by Penleigh Boyd, completed in 1921.

191

There are great views over Weeroona Bay and towards Portsea jetty. Now walk towards the park entrance and pick up the right hand path that heads back towards Portsea Village. The next 'painting' is at 'The Cutting' (map 156 E2 in your Melways). This painting is accessed by turning right and walking about 100 metres towards the jetty. This walk takes you past the colourful boat sheds and onto the walking path behind the rock seawall. You will see the next painting by Penleigh Boyd near the start of this seawall. Continue walking towards the jetty and then back to the main road. Walk past the hotel until you reach Franklin Road. Turn left, passing the Portsea Camp, down a gravel road. Bear right to the start of the walking track (known as 'millionaires walk' for the magnificent properties which abut the cliffs and foreshore along this highly prized piece of real estate.

Walking along this unmade path, approximately one hundred metres from the end of the road, there is a fork in the path. Take the left hand fork near a house with a large flagpole, you are now at Barrett's Point. Sir Arthur Streeton painted this delightful scene in 1920. The next artists paintings are located at Point King, about 1500 metres towards Sorrento.

Continue walking until you arrive at Shelly Beach and pick up a track back to Point Nepean Road. Then proceed along the wide pathway to Point King Road. Walk down Point King Road picking up the walking track which will take you to the next view point. There is a memorial plaque and cairn, as well as a flagpole at Point King. The plaque indicates that on the ninth of March 1802 acting Lieut John Murray took possession of Point King on behalf of her Majesty the Queen.

This viewpoint has two paintings. One by Arthur Boyd and the other by Sir Arthur Streeton. Continue along this 'exclusive' pathway. Again passing fantastic properties, complete with well maintained rolling lawns, flagpoles and the occasional swimming pool. There are a number of gates to walk through on this particular part of the walk. It can feel a little intimidating walking through these gates and walking very close to a number of private residences. Rest assured that this is a well worn path. The only thing you should adhere to is to abide by the sign:

Portsea Sorrento Artists Trail.

'Please shut the gate'. At Point King there is yet another impressive work by Arthur Streeton.

Continue on your walk now, again passing through gateways. You are approaching Lentell Avenue where a painting by Ray Hodgkinson is featured. From Lenttel Avenue walk back towards point Nepean Road pick up the path and head towards Sorrento and the Sorrento Historic Park This is a great park for a picnic, particularly if there are families with young children. There are swings and playground equipment, barbecues and a rotunda in this delightfully maintained community asset. A number of the trees here have plaques highlighting species information. Continue walking past the amenities block out towards the viewing area overlooking the bay adjacent to Sorrento pier. Another artists display, by Roland Clark, is featured near the entrance to Sorrento Pier between the toilet block and the foreshore. Another view by the same artist is actually located at the end of the Sorrento Pier.

Before concluding your walk, take the time to investigate the remains of the old Sorrento tram track and station a few metres above the roadway and opposite the amenities block. This former tram terminus has excellent images highlighting Sorrento earlier last century. I was particularly impressed with the old images of Sorrento Ocean Beach. The author spent a number of years on surf patrol at this location.

If you are keen on local history make sure you visit the Sorrento Museum located in Old Melbourne Rd Sorrento.

Note: The name **Artists Trail** is somewhat misleading as there is no clearly defined pathway that links up with the 14 different works displayed.

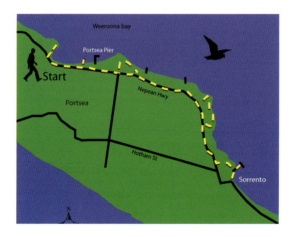

RED HILL TO MERRICKS TRAIL

A great walk, partly on the former railway line to Red Hill. This is a quiet trail which will put some serious kilometres under your belt. Enjoy panoramic views of vineyards and farms, Westernport Bay and the rolling Mornington Peninsula countryside.

Start	Callanans Road, Red Hill
Distance	13+ kilometres return
Time	Allow 5 - 6 hours return
Effort	Medium
Maps	Melways map 191 B7
When	Anytime

Head out in an easterly direction through the Redhill Bushland Reserve on a wide, well maintained and relatively flat path which is on part of the old railway route. Initially the forest provides much shelter. Notice small tree ferns on the left hand side as you leave the rear of the Redhill Trading Company building.

The track is now heading in an easterly direction and slowly descending as it meets Tonkins Road. This is an 'easy walking' track. The Red Hill to Merricks section on the walk is largely flat and downhill so effort is graded at easy to medium. The return leg will give walkers a more solid workout.

There is little navigation required by walkers as the path is wide, well signposted and conducive to having a good talk with your walking

Red Hill to Merricks Rail Trail.

friends. This is the type of walk where you can walk for a number of kilometres without realizing that you have covered so much ground. It's similar to a walk on a long sandy beach where there is only one direction in which to walk and you can move along easily, looking at the scenery and enjoying the great outdoors.

The track is in good condition, even during winter and should present little difficulty to walkers.

Signage will direct you to the next part of the trail, beyond Tonkins Road. It is 3.5 kilometres to Merricks .

A small hill is encountered with views of the hinterland, Sandy Point and Westernport Bay. The track is now rougher underfoot but still very serviceable. The trail still continues, bearing east, until within 750 metres of Merricks/Red Hill Station ground, the direction changes to southeast before terminating at the Merricks/Red Hill Station ground.

My suggestion is to head for the Merricks General Store and a café stop before starting the return journey. Alternatively, use a car shuttle to return to the beginning of the walk. I had arranged a car pickup at Merricks for my 'return' journey to Red Hill.

The railway line ceased operations over 50 years ago.

Note: This trail is open to bike riders, horses, joggers and walkers. Parts of this trail are suitable for strollers.

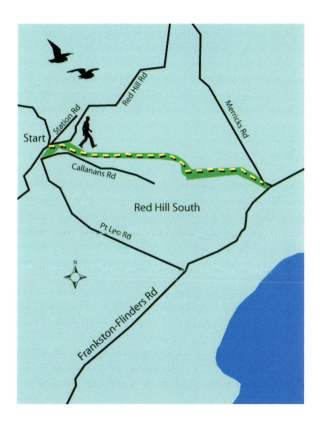

SAFETY BEACH TO DROMANA AND ANTHONY'S NOSE

A walk for families with young children, or a leisurely stroll with a group of friends. This hike features a number of options including beach walking, using the recently upgraded foreshore walking track and bike path or even taking the footpath through the retail precinct of Dromana to check out the numerous retail outlets and cafes. Other options include utilising one of the numerous barbecue and picnic facilities as well as children's play grounds en route!

Start	Mt Martha Sailing Club carpark
Distance	6 kilometres one way
Time	Allow 2 hours one way
Effort	Easy to medium
Maps	Melways map 150 E11
When	Anytime

Start near the Safety Beach Sailing Club. Information signage near the club rooms offers reasons as to the naming of this beach. One of the early settlers, on trying to land provisions from a sailing ketch, ran aground on a sand bar but was fortunately able to push the boat off with assistance. The sailor was John Aitken and the vessel was the Chill. The information board also describes the influence of the Bunerong People, traditional owners of the area.

The gravel walking track which runs between the beach and the main road is easy to pick up. As you approach the Volunteer Coast Guard building there is a small 'dog-leg' in the track before the walk continues on a concrete path. Passing the boat ramp the path again becomes well formed gravel and continues through the foreshore. There are two elevated sections of the track, both constructed of timber, which add some interest to the walk. There are some strategically placed seats adjacent to the walking path and these may well be the opportunity to rest and take a photo or re-group your walking party.

This section of the track terminates near an amenities block adjacent to Prescott Avenue. From here the options are to continue on the grassed foreshore area or to take to the sandy beach. Weather conditions and prevailing winds will no doubt influence your decision.

There is no track until point Nepean Road is reached. It is approximately 3 kilometres from the sailing club to Nepean Highway.

Dromana Life Saving Club.

From the Point Nepean Road intersection there is an excellent path which winds its way through the foreshore. There is some vegetative cover here. Trees and scrub, some of which has been replanted, all add to the your experience as you head towards the Dromana shopping centre precinct. On a midsummer's weekend the pedestrian traffic became decidedly busier as we approached Dromana Jetty and the Dromana Lifesaving Club. Lifesavers were in attendance on this picturesque summer's afternoon. There are over 20,000 volunteer lifesavers throughout Australia.

Families, a few bike riders and teenagers were all making the most of the sunny afternoon. There are barbecues and picnic tables, seats, and some rooved picnic shelters as well as fresh water taps. You cannot help but notice the shops and cafes nearby that always tempt walkers of any age.

Almost opposite the jetty is an excellent adventure playground which would have to be a logical stopping point for any family walkers with young children.

To the west of the lifesaving club are more well maintained barbecue facilities, picnic shelters and seats. As we moved away from the central business hub the path became a little quieter and less concentration was required as we walked ever closer towards Anthonys Nose.

I must make mention of the Dromana Visitor Information Centre. For residents and visitors alike, this facility has a wealth of information, continually updated. The ever friendly staff can advise on walking tracks, accommodation, wineries points of interest, fishing charters and the like. I am sure you will find something of interest here. The painted gum leaves, framed and with a strong aboriginal influence really took my eye when I last called in here. I had never seen anything quite like them before.

As you continue on the path towards Anthonys Nose, there are some slow points, designed for cyclists to dismount. Walkers need to take care and be observant wherever there are any blind spots or forward visibility is limited.

Soon enough you will pass the Dromana Boat Hire shed and shortly after this the path terminates at the beginning of the caravan and camping area. You are still able to walk through a camping area but the beach is always an additional option when you reach the boat ramp. Just before Anthonys Nose you will have walked almost exactly 6 km. This is where your rendezvous vehicle is ready to pick you up or return on the same path. Either way I hope you enjoyed your walk.

A fit or power walker could undertake this total distance, one way, in around one hour. Walkers with families or in groups could take well over 2 hours with stops.

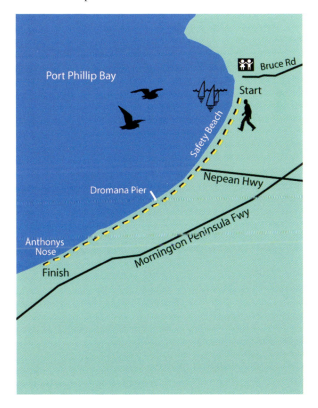

SEAWINDS TO SEAMIST DRIVE ARTHURS SEAT

This walk takes you on a small section of the Two Bays Walking Track and is well within the capabilities of all walkers. Easy on the feet, easy on the eye, sheltered from sun and wind, this walk takes in the views from Arthurs Seat and the Seawinds lookout. Make this venue a 'must visit' location.

Start	Seawinds carpark, Arthurs Seat
Distance	4.8 kilometres return (2.2 kilometres one way)
Time	1+ hours
Grade	Easy to medium
Map	Melways 159 D11
When	Almost anytime except Code Red Days
Suggestion	Car pickup at Seamists Drive

Seawinds is a magical name for a magical location. The renowned William Ricketts sculptures have achieved international acclaim and the delightful gardens, top class facilities and views all make this one of the best parks on the peninsula. The views of the bay are spectacular and on a clear day you can see the Otways and Mt Macedon, features that are over 100 kilometres away. Picnic facilities here beckon the visitor to stay awhile and perhaps you will.

The walking track from Arthurs Seat and the Seawinds picnic area is well signposted. It starts as a wide gravel track and winds its way from the manicured gardens into a more forested area. As you walk along the path the first intersection is only 200 metres away. One path will take

Seawinds, Arthurs Seat.

you to the T. C. McKellar Reserve and a circuit walk. Take the right hand path which is the continuation of the Two Bays Walking Track. Signage along the route is informative and highlights various aspects of the flora and fauna of the National Park. The path becomes more of a bushwalking track as it narrows, the surface is now less gravelled, and tree roots and stones must be negotiated. The track is still very easy to walk along. You are simply moving away from the vestiges of 'civilisation' into a more 'natural environment. I would be surprised if you did not hear the sounds of birds on this section of the walk. Stopping and waiting for a short while to listen for any forest dwellers may surprise you.

About 1 kilometre from the last track intersection with the T.C. McKellar Walk is another track junction. The junction heads left to Seamists Drive and to King's Waterfall which is around 800 metres away.

Take the wide management vehicle track out to Seamists Drive to pick up your other vehicle or simply return the way you came.

If this walk is one of your first forays into 'bushwalking' it may well 'wet your appetite' to take on longer and more adventurous walks. It may seem a simple thing to extend this walk, perhaps attempting Kings Falls, which is not far away. Remember you usually have to return the same way and if you are leading the group ensure that you have assessed the capabilities and comfort of all in your party. Often the return leg of a hike seems longer for some reason. I've never investigated the psychology behind this phenomenon. Interestingly enough some websites claim the reverse is true but I maintain that fatigue and a slower walking pace may prolong the return walking times. Some of your group may fatigue earlier and not enjoy the walk because they have over-extended themselves. If everyone enjoys the experience they will certainly come back for more.

SHOREHAM TO FLINDERS

Peaceful and remote, with your destination visible and lying in wait at the end of your coastal foray, this shoreline walk affords changing views of Westernport Bay as well as great views of Phillip Island and Bass Strait. For maximum enjoyment only attempt on sunny days, low tides and warm temperatures. This walk is a buzz.

Start	The Pines car park, Shoreham
Distance	11+ kms return.
Time	3 hours walking time
Grade	Easy
Maps	Melways Map 256 F10
When	Any season. Low tide preferred. Avoid SE winds over 15 knots
Suggestion	Lunch or café stop at Flinders. A car shuttle may be an option.

An old favourite of mine since my surfing days at Point Leo, this part of the coast is laid back and less hurried than the mainstream beaches of the Peninsula. There is no public access to the coast between Shoreham and Flinders so the walker will enjoy a trek that is unencumbered by civilisation.

Before heading out check the signage on the flora and fauna of the area, including the weedy sea dragon. We started walking on a sunny winters' day accompanied by a light tail wind to speed us along. With an anticipated temperature of around 17C and lots of blue sky this was a magnificent day for coastal walking.

Shoreham to Flinders.

You can take the beach or the roadway almost to the end of the first headland, due south of the carpark. After negotiating the first rocky headland there is another hundred metres of sand before some more water worn rock has to be traversed. The rock or gravel sections of this walk require a little more care but will not be too arduous. We reached around 6 kilometres per hour over the sand but with weed and rock hopping that figure slowed down to less than 5 kilometres per hour.

There are some larger and higher rocks to traverse further along the beach. You can readily discern the distinctive orange lichen of this rocky outcrop, the colour being very similar to rocks at Martha Point on the other side of the Mornington Peninsula. With only a few footprints on the beach there is little pedestrian traffic here. This is a quiet coastal walk well away from most of the tell-tale signs of habitation. There are one or two houses on the clifftops en route to Flinders, but otherwise the peaceful farming land, Westernport Bay and Phillip Island will be your walking companions.

Abalone shell.

I took note that the highest tides had obviously inundated the fore dune so this would almost be a 'no-go zone' under such conditions. The next small point looms large and numerous banksia trees were showing the white underside of their leaves as a light northerly wind continued to blow. More loose gravel, which is easily traversed, was negotiated again. This is the pattern of this walk all the way to Flinders. Sand, gravel, headlands and some seaweed banks. I suggest keeping up higher on the beach and closer to the vegetative area, where the gravel is usually smaller in size, firmer underfoot and easier to walk.

Passing some steps, these are on private property, the beach is now largely gravelled again and the walking speed again will be reduced. An electric fence, some of which was on a freshly eroded section of beach, is evident. Ensure you keep young and inquisitive children away from this potential hazard. As you round the point you can see Flinders Jetty in the distance and on this occasion the distinctive orange-coloured Westernport Bay pilot boat.

With sand underfoot for another few hundred metres, it is easy to average up to 7 kilometres per hour for fit walkers. This particular section of beach had numerous shells including the distinctive abalone shells.

A couple of penguins were washed up on the beach here and this is not too surprising as the penguin colony at Phillip Island is probably around less than 10 kilometres distant and these amazing small birds have been known to forage to 40 kilometres a day from their burrows.

Approximately halfway between Flinders and Shoreham is Manton Creek. During the winter season crossing this water course may necessitate the removal of the footwear. I traversed water to a depth of 200 mm on a falling tide. Just beyond the creek was an amazing sight with possibly 20 to 30 hooded plover taking flight. These birds were obviously very timid. I have not seen as many hooded plover in one location for quite some time on the Mornington Peninsula.

Approaching another headland, there are three quite distinguishable pines clinging to the cliff face. As you round this point Flinders Jetty comes into full view as well as a number of dwellings perched above the cliffs. Another sighting of more shore birds included black swans and two pied oyster catchers together with seven sooty oyster catchers. There was also one solitary Ibis and possibly up to 50 silver gulls with perhaps 20 pacific gulls and a pair of white faced herons. Binoculars may be useful here.

Notice the large yellow navigational pole to seaward, the distinctive outline of West Head and the naval station which bears due south. Coming closer to Flinders Jetty there is now a sandy beach for most of the way which gives you a good ground speed. The township of Flinders makes its presence felt with housing perched above you. Within half a kilometre of the jetty there are considerable mounds of the fine seaweed, some perhaps up to a metre and a half high. These miniature headlands of seaweed will obviously move depending upon tides and wind directions. A small creek, within 200 metres of the jetty, should present little obstacle. Notice the adjacent foot track which heads out to the road. Continue on the beach until the jetty is reached.

The total distance one way was 5.3 kilometres on the GPS. Return the same way or await your vehicle pickup. Alternatively head up to the Flinders retail area for that coffee and lunch stop.

This walk is best attempted on lower tide levels. As with all coastal walks, Easter time, with its king tides, will make progress somewhat more problematic but not impossible. Low tides will invariably expose more beach sand and make for a quicker and easier walk. While I covered this distance in 1 hour, larger walking groups, families and those wanting a restful walk will take up to twice as long and still get to enjoy what is a great coastal walk.

Enthusiastic walkers may want to start at Point Leo and add three kilometres and 45 minutes one way, to their walk.

SHOREHAM TO POINT LEO

The serenity of Shoreham with its small cliffs and tall trees are in contrast to the wide sandy beaches and low coastal vegetation as you make your way towards Point Leo. Easy walking.

Start	The Pines car park, Shoreham
Distance	Up to 7 kms return.
Time	2+ hours walking time
Grade	Easy
Maps	Melways Map 256 F10
When	Any season. Low tide for easier walking.

Shoreham is a low-key, sedate 'village' on the shores of Westernport Bay. Time seems to pass more slowly here and while keen walkers will make good speed over the firm sand the 'time dilation' is evident. No one seems in a rush. The 'hustle and bustle' is on the other side of the bay at Sorrento and Rye, especially in the summer months.

Leave your vehicle at the 'Pines foreshore carpark. Head due north, passing Stony Creek, which will present little problem unless there has been heavy rain or there is a high tide. At high tide this creek could be 1 metre deep so make your plans accordingly. Parts of this beach are very similar to Tanners Bay on the west coast of Flinders Island where paper nautilus shells are washed onto the beach from time to time. (See Walks of Flinders Island by K. Martin)

Passing under the cliffs, with extensive stands of pines trees, notice the fine seaweed that is washed up along this section of coastline. This

Shoreham to Point Leo.

seaweed is indicative of low wave and tidal action. Walking past the small headlands and the Shoreham camping area the beach becomes wide and expansive, especially at low tide. There are extensive rock platforms here. Honey Suckle Reef is a much frequented surfing venue when conditions are suitable. The sand here is ideal for strollers and children's bikes and certainly makes for good traction for keen walkers wanting to build up some speed. Walkers with young families who wish to make a shorter walk could consider starting their walk from the end of Nelson Street, although some steps need to be negotiated.

The Point Leo headland and the surf club patrol tower are the prominent features to the northeast. The vast rock platforms and extensive mounds of seaweed give this coastal area a distinctive feel from the scoured ocean beaches between Flinders, Cape Schanck and Point Nepean.

As you walk along this beach keep an eye on the margin between the seaweed and sand. Occasionally this area will have interesting items washed up on to the shoreline. Perhaps a sea urchin shell or a small crayfish shell and even part of an old fishing rod. Colourful limpet shells and small abalone shells are part of the scene here. Patches of pink seaweed are also washed up onto this beach, this type of seaweed being similar to that harvested on King Island in western Bass Strait.

Take in the views towards Phillip Island and the headland at Seal Rocks. The foreshore is somewhat similar to the Waratah Bay to Walkerville coastline with banksias being one of the dominant tree species. Notice

Stony Creek, Shoreham.

small dry creek beds which have been washed by the high tides. There is often a certain amount of debris which is washed into these scoured areas.

Your walk continues until you reach the Point Leo beach and its facilities. Wander up to the point and around the headland, Bobbanaring Point, if you have the time and inclination. Or leave this walk and exploration of Point Leo for another day. (See walk no. 44) Again king tides such as experienced at Easter and big surf can present a different situation where the waves actually come right up to the fore dune. Return the same way.

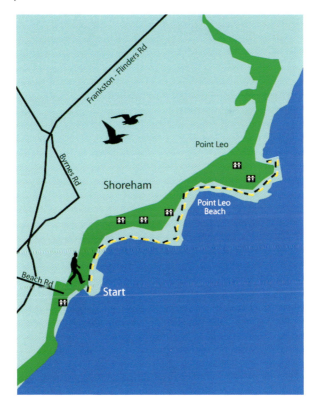

SOMERS TO SANDY POINT

Walk into the wilderness on a long, quiet, beach. Wind in your hair, waves lapping the shore. This long haul beach walk also offers views to Cowes, Phillip Island and Westernport Bay.

Start	Car park, Corner Belvedere and Miramar Roads
Distance	Up to 10 kilometres return
Time	Two hours
Effort	Medium
Maps	Melways Map 194 F11
When	Low tide required

Ample parking is available at the end of Belvedere Road. A stairway of over 100 steps will take you past holiday homes and beach houses and down to the beach. You should instantly feel a sense of relief as you head into the wide open spaces and make out for Sandy Point, to your left and due east.

There is something special about starting out on a long beach walk with an objective clearly in sight. There is not much to contend with except, perhaps, some fallen trees or large pieces of driftwood. The freedom of a beach, its simplicity and restfulness, the ebb and flow of the tide, all make for a mentally relaxing experience. There is the uncluttered and uncomplicated nature of a beach that will always appeal to free and roaming spirits and beachcombers alike.

As you will readily see, this part of the Westernport coastline has been subject to heavy erosion over recent years and high tides may make

Somers to Sandy Point.

progress out towards Sandy Point very difficult if not impossible without some serious

tree hopping and scrub bashing. Make sure you are well prepared for this walk. Take adequate supplies in your day pack for sun and rain, depending on your forecast. Keep a lookout for any interesting flotsam and jetsam. Banded birds occasionally wash up on beaches and please report any identifying bands to Parks Victoria.

With firm sand underfoot and a light wind, perhaps a tail-wind from the southwest, good walkers will make the slow sweep of Sandy Point within the hour. If I am walking with a group I always like to stop every half hour, on the half hour, for a break and re-grouping, if required.

While there will be little variation on this coastal walk, the township of Cowes and Phillip Island will loom larger as you approach the point.

The occasional pleasure craft and ship may also be seen on Westernport Bay. Over the summer months sailing is a serious activity in this part of the bay and there are a large number of devotees honing their skills and plying for a place at race time. The colourful sails and craft always make for added interest.

For autumn and early winter walkers this long beach walk may offer the chance of finding an illusive paper nautilus shell which has been washed up onto the beach. These prized shells are very distinctive. My first nautilus shell was found at Flinders many years ago. I initially thought my find was some type of Japanese artefact such was its ornamental nature, its simplicity and its uniqueness. It is said these shells come up onto beaches every seven years but there is certainly no hard and fast rule. Good luck!

Shorebirds.

As you negotiate the sweep of Sandy Point, French Island will come into view. You are surprisingly close to the island, which is only three kilometres away. I would advise against swimming here as strong currents may make for a dangerous situation. As well, you are now some distance from help, if required.

The return walk should present little difficulty unless there is an incoming or flood tide. Take care with surging waves, particularly with strong southeast winds. As a precaution, I like to place all electronic gear in strong, zip-lock bags.

I always like to put places like Sandy Point on my walking agenda as it is a geographical feature which makes for a 'turning pojnt' on the map. Something akin to walking out to 'Lands End' in southwest England, I imagine. Cape Schanck is another nearby location that also marks a major change of direction. I guess the bottom line here is to do the walk and experience the feel of this location for yourself.

Note: This beach is a designated leash free area.

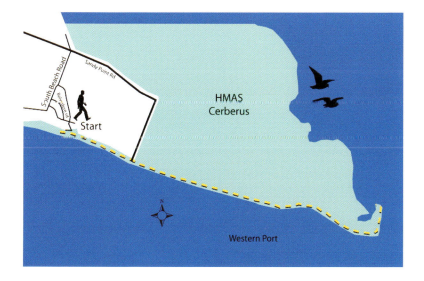

SORRENTO OCEAN BEACH AND ROCKPOOLS

> *Popular for well over 100 years, Sorrento continues to attract visitors. The rugged ocean beach, flanked by cliffs and rock stacks is very impressive. The sandy beach offers just enough room for that refreshing swim over the summer months when the beach is patrolled. The enchanting rockpools never fail to interest people of all ages.*

Start	Sorrento Ocean Beach Carpark
Distance	2 kilometres return
Time	Allow up to 2 hours
Effort	Easy to medium, steps and stairways
Maps	Melways Map 156 J9
When	Low tide required

Ample parking is available at the ocean beach and this should be an easy task except at peak holiday times. Start your walk by passing the Sorrento Surf Life Saving Club and taking time to read the informative signage before you descend the stairway to the beach. At low tide there are extensive rock platforms and your progress along the short sandy beach will be easy. There is a large rockpool here which is a favourite for swimmers over the warmer months. Continue around the small cliffy headland on the flatter rock platform. There is a rough path just below the cliff which involves some rock-hopping.

Rockpools can contain a diverse array of creatures. Remember that this is part of the national park. All flora and fauna is protected.

Sorrento Ocean Beach.

Within 5 to 10 minutes you will have arrived at the next sandy beach. Again, low tide gives the walker a good margin of safety. Incoming tides with large swell and high tide levels can push the sea right up to the rocks on this small headland.

If you decide to venture onto the rock platforms take particular care. Large waves can break here at any time. When I was on surf patrol here a few years ago nine visitors from Melbourne all suffered cuts and abrasions after a large wave washed the family group onto the rocks! Strong south westerly and off-shore winds can result in larger waves breaking close to the shore.

Continue now towards the feature known as Sphinx Rock, some half a kilometre distant. The walk along the beach is easy going although it can be a hot walk on a summer's day. Take water and your daypack, even on short walks such as this. Aim for the stairway at the end of this section of beach which takes some effort but gives the walker great views of the coastline as you climb towards the track. The stairways are a good workout and if you are not used to climbing stairs, take your time, pause at the platforms between the runs of stairs. A slow and steady pace will get you there.

Coppins Lookout, the rotunda that looks like a round, Asian straw hat, is perhaps the most recognizable feature along this section of coast. This is your next stop. From the lookout it is an easy task to walk down to the carpark. The café and kiosk may tempt you and there are also barbecue facilities and an amenities block here.

Only swim between the flags at this or any ocean beach on the Mornington Peninsula.

This walk could certainly be extended to Portsea Ocean Beach, which is just over 1.5 kilometres from Sphinx Rock. Again, check tide levels and be well equipped, even on short haul walks.

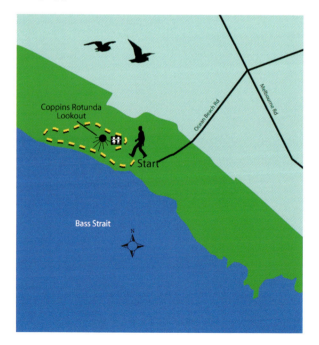

SORRENTO TO BLAIRGOWRIE

Take in Victoria's historic Collins settlement, an inland and coastal route, see moored boats, seven jetties and delightfully sheltered, picturesque bays and campers in season. This walk has plenty to keep you interested.

Start	The Baths or Rotunda, Sorrento
Distance	8+ kms circuit.
Time	Allow up to 3 hours
Grade	Easy to medium
Maps	Melways map 157 B7
When	Choose low tide to coincide with your beach walk
Suggestion	A picnic en route or café stop at Blairgowrie

Variation is the key on this 'must do' walk. From sandy beaches to the rocky headlands of the Sisters there is much to keep the mind active. The inland route is undulating, taking in some really good lookouts and vantage points. This walk lends itself to a partial circuit trek which negates the need to walk on the beach both ways.

Your walk starts near the Sorrento ferry terminal or the baths café and continues along the beach until a timber and steel fence is reached. Proceed through the fence and pick up the walking track adjacent to a plaque at the Sorrento camping ground: Bunurong Baluk Walk, which recognizes the original inhabitants of the area. The inland track from here ascends some timber steps and continues through coastal vegetation behind the caravan and camping area. Initially the track

Sorrento to Blairgowrie.

was somewhat overgrown when I last did this walk. Soon enough you will reach a high point which has great views towards Arthurs Seat, Sorrento beach, the jetty and moored pleasure craft adjacent to the Sorrento Sailing Couta Boat Club. The walking track eventually meets a roadway which takes you behind the club where there is a top-class picnic area complete with barbecue, multiple picnic tables and very well-kept lawns. The view from this picnic area overlooks the jetty and a plethora of yachts and boats moored nearby.

Continue on the roadway, now gravel, passing a walkers and cyclists sign. The path now continues behind a number of residential properties between the beach and Point Nepean Road. This part of the walk is sheltered perhaps from showers, summer sun or strong winds. Presently there is a fork in the track. Take the left hand track towards Settlement Point. Soon there is another viewpoint. Take time to walk into the exclusive and intimate Sullivans Bay, perhaps one of most delightful beaches along this part of the coast. Being flanked by the West and East Sisters rocky headlands, Sullivan Bay is quite a unique experience. Perhaps this would be a perfect spot for a swim in the warmer weather.

Pick up the track again passing the 'tide ways' residence where you skirt point Nepean Road and walk through the former Oaks entry posts. Continue on the sealed road until you reach the Bicentennial Memorial for the Collins Settlement 1803 -2003. Take the time to read interesting details associated with this historic area. From here pick up the signposted entry and path way into Collins Settlement. There are extensive information boards and images here. Take the slowly ascending path up to the four early settlers graves, passing Fawkner Lookout which has magnificent views of Camerons Bight the Blairgowrie Yacht Squadron and the beaches towards Whitecliffs and Arthurs Seat. There is another lookout at the top of this hill to visit before returning down past the Information Centre and back onto the track. From these viewpoints you can surmise the route around the coast and back to Sorrento, which necessitates low tides.

Continue on the roadway, past the Bicentennial Memorial which now parallels Point Nepean Road. The track and minor roadway head past the small jetty at Camerons Bight. There is another small walking track to pick up on your left just as you approach the main road. This leads to another camping area where you take the vehicular tracks. Continue on the camping road closest to the foreshore, passing an amenities block until a number of well maintained boat houses are seen. Take the small track behind these boat houses which meets with another vehicular access track. Again, pick up another walking track until you finally reach the main car park above the Blairgowrie Yacht Squadron. From here take the stairway down to the beach and continue along the beach until Blairgowrie where there is an amenities block and a variety of shops. This could be your café and lunch stop before embarking on the return journey.

Return the same way or for an alternative take the coastal and beach route. Again, you need a low tide, and tide tables are always a useful inclusion in any coastal walkers day pack. While the coastal route is less challenging navigationally, there is plenty to see from the perspective of sea level. While some walkers may want to summons their chauffeurs at Blairgowrie I would strongly recommend this circuit walk as a very interesting and challenging walk, at any time of the year.

The walking notes, above, may give the impression that the inland route to Blairgowrie is complicated. It is an easy walk and it's simply matter of following your instincts and using your navigational skills to pick up the next 'logical' path, roadway or track that keeps you headed in the general direction of Blairgowrie. If you do take a wrong turn you can always backtrack but you certainly will not get lost between the coastline and Point Nepean Road.

STAR WALK METEORS AND SATELLITES ALIVE

A 'must do' walk on a warm summer's night that may leave you breathless with the wonder of the 'heavens above'. 'As the stars in the heavens as the sand on the seashore*.' Highlights may include meteors and satellites.

Start	Anywhere away from street lights and towns.
Distance	2 kms
Time	After dusk and pre-dawn 20 mins to 2+ hours
Grade	Flat grade, smooth surface highly recommended, sandy beach
Maps	A star chart and meteor shower predictions could be useful. Smart phones now have apps that give you star positions
When	Anytime of the year. Wait for very clear skies with Magellan Clouds clearly discernible for optimal viewing.
Suggestion	Take binoculars

This walk can be a real treat if you are prepared to take a chance and walk on a dark road or beach on a star-spangled night. Even a pre-dawn walk is good too. Watch the sun-rise from the summit of your choice of hills. There is a real 'wow' factor here and country and coastal areas with their small number of street lights are conducive to a memorable experience if the sky is dark and clear.

Some tips for optimal viewing include having calm conditions where the salt spray and atmospheric haze is at a minimum. Having no moon or a new moon rising later can also be helpful. It is best to allow up

Southern Auroa. Photo courtesy of P. Skilton, MPAS.

to 20 minutes for your eyes to become accustomed to the dark. It takes this long for your pupils to fully dilate and to be able to see very faint objects. Making use of averted vision, whereby you do not look directly at an object but slightly away means that you will maximize the most light-sensitive part of the eye. (Your optic nerve connects directly behind your pupil and therefore this area is a little less sensitive to low light conditions than the outer part of your eye.) Averted vision is particularly useful when using binoculars.

Over a number of years the author has observed scores of meteors and satellites. (A local identity was heard to say that on any clear night you may see up to 5 satellites per hour!) Every year in early December there are 7 different meteor showers. While you may see only a few per night, three years ago the author counted eight meteors in the hour while walking along a dark road.

The zodiacal light is a cone shaped phenomenon (akin to something like an aurora) and the author witnessed this event one cold September morning in the eastern sky. Zodiacal light occurs when the sun illuminates the dust which is in the planetary plain. It is not a common event and is best seen from northern latitudes.

Take a star wheel if you have one and the Astronomical Almanac, which gives details of the planets, star positions and meteor showers. This can be of considerable use.

The most memorable event the author has witnessed was undoubtedly Comet McNaught in January 2007. Spending the best part of three hours walking nearly 6 kilometres to the intersection of a remote country road the huge twin tails of this spectacular comet were an amazing sight. One tail was a gas tail or wake and the other was an ion or solar wind tail! Walking continued until the comet's head or coma had set in the southwest around 1-00 am!

Another early morning beach walk gave rise to a most unusual sighting of the rising crescent moon, a 'spike of light' just emerging over the horizon. To all appearances the initial shaft of light was a short but very bright knife-edge Both the author and his daughter could not believe what they were seeing at first until this very fine crescent moon rose a few degrees above the horizon.

Iridium Flares are satellites that shine very brightly as the sun briefly reflects off the satellites' solar panels. The 'heavens above' website allows the observer to predict when these spectacular satellites will briefly flash in a dark sky. This is an amazing sight. See *www.heavens-above.com*

The sighting of the Larger and Lesser Magellan Clouds are good indicators that you have a dark sky. As well, if you can spot the Coal Sack, a dark area near the Southern Cross, then this too is an excellent indicator of optimal viewing conditions. The internet as well as your local library will have information and references for star-gazers! Good viewing!

Walkers interested in attending an open evening and observing night with a local astronomical group should visit *http://www.mpas.asn.au/* This is the website for the Mornington Peninsula Astronomical Society which I can highly recommend. The Starwalk App is also very useful.

TEA TREE CREEK FLINDERS

58

Rugged and windswept, remote and inhospitable, Tea Tree Creek, at its ocean terminus, can offer a glimpse of nature at its most powerful. The re-vegetated pathway offers a glimpse of the prolific bird life to be found in the area.

Start	Boneo Road Flinders, near Keys Road
Distance	Under 2 kilometres return
Time	30 minutes
Effort	Easy to medium
Maps	Melways Map 260 J10
When	Anytime. This is an exposed ocean location exercise extreme care. Low tide preferred.

Limited parking is directly adjacent to Boneo Road. Shortly after commencing your walk on a grassed track to the coastline you may be greeted with the sounds of many birds which frequent this re-vegetated area. The banksia seed pods are a favourite delicacy for many birds. Birds of prey are also part of the makeup of this area. I last walked here in autumn and a goss hawk or harrier was seen to fly off in the direction of the ocean with a smaller bird, perhaps a chick, firmly in its clutches. This was a dramatic event but it happened far too quickly for me to get the camera ready for an image.

The numerous Banksia trees which were in 'bloom' with their multiple seed pods were a great attraction for all types of birds. This whole precinct here is a great advertisement for the usefulness and general amenity offered to wildlife by extensive revegetation programs.

Derilict machinery at Tea Tree Creek.

The track down to the coast can be muddy in places after rain but it should not present any difficulty. Closer to the coastline a fence is encountered. Pass through the barrier. Continue on a track towards the coast. You are now passing the site of an old quarry. The derelict machinery here is evidence of these former activities.

A small stairway eventually leads you out to Cairns Bay. The coastline here is spectacular. It offers a small sandy beach which is unusual along this mainly rocky coast. Once at the beach walk out to the left or due east to investigate the large sand dune. Look for the easiest path along the shoreline. Often you can pick up a well-worn foot track that makes for easier and quicker walking, these rough tracks usually being higher up on the foreshore and closer to the vegetation. Trekking further along the shoreline you can venture out to the rock platform if conditions are safe. Your progress will eventually be halted by the sea as a deep channel runs right up to the cliff face here. Return the same way, looking for any interesting items washed up onto the beach.

The usual warnings apply here. Do not swim at this unpatrolled beach under any circumstances. Take particular care if surf is breaking on the shoreline. Surging waves can rise up many metres onto the shoreline without warning. On my last walk here I experienced three metre waves breaking offshore, making a spectacular sight but also heightening my awareness of a potentially dangerous situation. Take extreme care. Return the same way.

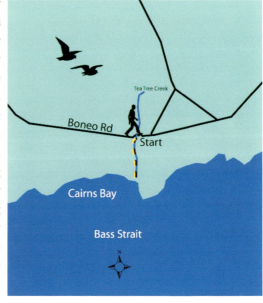

TOOTGAROOK WETLANDS

Tootgarook wetlands formed part of a larger swamp area that extended from Boneo through to Port Phillip Bay. Today, this important remnant habitat is home to numerous animals including frogs and birds. A short walk, but interesting for its habitat values.

Start	Tern Avenue, Rosebud West
Distance	0.5 kilometres
Time	Under 30 minutes
Grade	Flat, easy
Map	Melways Map 169 E5
When	Anytime

On arrival at Tootgarook Wetlands you should be greeted with the sound of frogs. Biologists tell us that frogs are an important indicator of the health of the environment. Proceed through the gate, this short walk takes you around the larger part of the perimeter of the swamp. This is a peaceful area which gives the walker a chance to observe some of the birds which inhabit the area. One of the more impressive dwellers in this 'wetland area' is the Ibis, a prehistoric looking bird with a long, pronounced curved beak.

Keep to the left-hand paths as you circumnavigate the wetlands. One side track takes you to a boardwalk which extends out into the swamp itself. There is the occasional seat en route and as you continue in an anti-clockwise direction you will pass a small bird hide open to the public on the eastern side of the wetlands area. Before long, the walking

Tootgarook Wetlands.

path terminates at Howqua Drive. Here you must bear left, continuing on the road to Kingfisher Avenue and then into Tern Avenue again, where you commenced the walk.

The prolonged multi-year drought which has severely affected south-eastern Australia, also took it toll on this wetland. The reeds have all but covered the swamp. However, in 2011, after the substantial summer rains, water is to be seen everywhere. One would expect that more birds will return to this area over time. It may be worthwhile to return to these wetlands from time to time, to check on the progress of local bird population. The large bird hide near the western entrance is presently closed to the public. Literature mentions that more than 100 different birds species can frequent this area

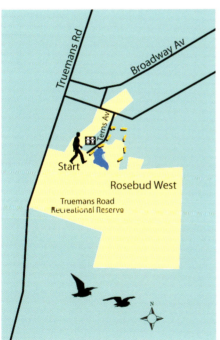

A longer walk could start at the junction of Point Nepean and Truemans Road (Map 169 E3), walking for one kilometre along the 'nature strip' on either side of Truemans Road until Ibis Grove and the Truemans Road Recreational Reserve is reached. From here it is a straightforward walk due east and into the wetlands area.

On my last visit to the wetlands the track was in need of some maintenance but still very useable. It would be great to see the track extended around the northern perimeter of the wetlands so that there was a continuous path within the wetlands area.

WATERFALL CREEK BUSHLAND RESERVE

Short, stimulating and with minimal effort required, anyone can undertake this walk on a relatively flat well-formed path. This reserve is particularly suitable for families with young children as you will find the self-guided walk has plenty to keep everyone interested.

Start	Corner Elizabeth Drive and Rosebud Avenue, Rosebud
Distance	Approx 1 Kilometre return
Time	20 minutes
Grade	Easy
Maps	Melways Map 170 G5
When	Almost anytime. Avoid on total fire ban days.
Suggestion	For families with children

Commence walking at the Rosebud Avenue entrance, near the intersection of Elizabeth Drive. The footwear-cleaning facility found at either entrance to the walk aims to reduce the incidence of cinnamon fungus, which has become a problem within parts of this reserve. Signage here indicates the fungus is an increasing problem.

This walking track features a number of points of interest, some seats and an informative brochure can usually be obtained from the boxes at either end of this trail. This interesting trek takes you through some dense natural vegetation including a creek, which flows readily after rain. The associated website indicates that frogs, koalas and even the

Waterfall Creek Bushland Reserve.

occasional echidna can be observed here. I have been impressed by the number of different bird calls as I wandered through this relic of native scrubland. While the walk is very close to residential development, the sensation is of being many kilometres away from civilization. Come and experience this 'surprise'.

Points of interest include:

The convergence of a number of vegetative communities with melaleucas, eucalypts, banksia and grass trees being prominent. This variation is thought to be explained by the converging of different soil types that give a rich base suitable for a wide range of flora;

The second point of interest includes the delightful Waterfall Creek, complete with a small wooden bridge. You may see delicate maiden hair and fishbone ferns. The fourth stop highlights local plants including Cherry Ballart, Banksias and the Native Clematis.

The pine trees near the number 5 post were planted by Rosebud Primary School students over half a century ago but are now classied as 'weeds'. Possibly, over time, these 'weeds' will be removed so that the native vegetation can more completely regain its lost ground in this location.

Also notice the nesting box high up in the prominent eucalypt near stop number five. Another of the animals found here includes the sugar glider. From post number 5 continue on the left hand track which takes you toward the tennis club. Post 7 indicates the birds inhabiting

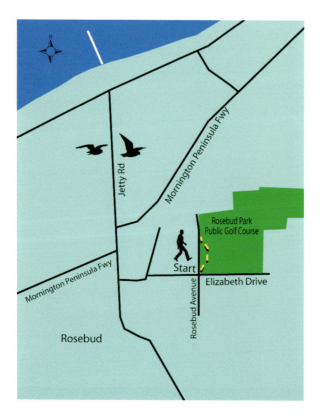

the reserve include the crested shrike-tit, white eared honey-eater and the superb fairy wren.

Grass trees, xanthorrhoea australis, were important to the original inhabitants and are now an enduring symbol of the Mornington Peninsula. The walk ends at the Rosebud Tennis Club and the options here are to return via the new trail or walk west along Hove Road to Rosebud Avenue before returning to your vehicle. Do not dismiss this small walk as insignicant. It is another small gem in the rich tapestry of the peninsula's environment.

Friends of Waterfall Creek Bushland must be thanked for maintaining this interesting walking venue. Please note the SPIFFA website has links to '40 bird calls' and this site is highly recommended. *www.spiffa.org*

At the time of writing, good summer rains had led to a profusion of bracken fern growth along the track and there was some impediment to our progress.

WHITECLIFFS, RYE TO BLAIRGOWRIE

61

An easy walk where you cannot get lost. Boat sheds and campers in season. Investigate the historic limestone kiln. Boats and water sports will all be there over the summer months. Or experience the cool and quieter times of the year when you may have the beach to yourself.

Start	Whitecliffs, opposite Minnimurra Street, Rye
Distance	6 kilometres return
Time	2 hours
Effort	Easy
Maps	Melways map 168 D3
When	Almost anytime. Very high tides will necessitate walking on the foreshore.

This interesting walk starts at the western end of the Rye foreshore camping area. Walk into the small reserve where a limestone kiln has been faithfully restored. Signage gives the walker an appreciation of the former activities in this area. This kiln is very similar to the more extensive kilns at Walkerville South in South Gippsland. Take the path out to the beach. Head up the stairway to the vantage point at the top of Whitecliffs. There are seats here and a wooden viewing deck. Binoculars are useful here. On a clear day the CBD skyline, Mt Macedon and Mt Dandenong will all be visible. There is an old Trig. Point here, now made obsolete with GPS technology. The seawall below was constructed early last century. Do not venture beyond the fence line as the sandstone cliffs are unstable.

Limestone kiln at Whitecliffs.

Having descended to the beach make your way due west towards Blairgowrie. The camping area and colourful boat sheds buzz with activity from December to Easter but at other times of the year you may be lucky to see just a handful of people on the beach. I have counted close to 40 boats moored opposite the camping area in peak holiday periods. There will be surf skis, jet skis, kayaks and all sorts of 'watercraft' to add interest to your walk during these busier times.

On high tides parts of the section of beach, near Whitecliffs, are impassable unless you are prepared to get your feet wet. The options for walkers are to walk along the beach to Blairgowrie or walk through the camping area, picking up the walking track which meanders its way through the foreshore vegetation before terminating near Canterbury Jetty Road. The foreshore walking track has been extensively revegetated

Sunrise at Rye.

in recent years and it is now showing the benefits of this program. One 'major' feature along the route is the Tyrone Boat Ramp. Between Whitecliffs and Tyrone Boat Ramp there is a single wooden lookout at a high point on the inland track. This is another great vantage point. Past the boat ramp the walking track meaders through a sheltered forest of Moonah trees, which have 'protected' status on the Mornington Peninsula.

Further along the bay shoreline, more boat sheds are in evidence. Whichever way you decide to walk you should arrive at Blairgowrie ready for the obligatory café stop. Blairgowrie is well endowed with an array of cafes from which to choose.

An alternative return route back to Whitecliffs can be made by taking a rough walking track between Point Nepean Road and the houses adjacent to the road. This return alternative may be handy if it is a very

Whitecliffs Rye.

hot or windy day. The track is well cleared in places but you will have to exercise discretion and use minor roadways, driveways and other access as appropriate. This 'alternative' path tracks all the way across the top of Whitecliffs and finishes at Minnimurra Street, the starting point for your walk. This 'track' is not featured on the Melways maps.

A new walking pathway has been constructed from Blairgowrie to Canterbury Jetty Road but it may be way too close to vehicular traffic for those preferring a quieter walk.

Because there are two and sometimes three alternative walking routes from Rye to Blairgowrie you may wish to consider weather conditions, such as how hot and sunny it is and the wind strength, direction and speed before choosing your route. Even light rain showers may necessitate conducting part of your walk through the more sheltered parts of the foreshore.

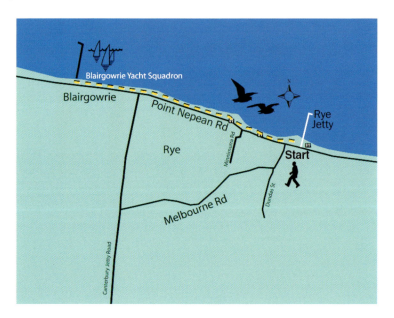

WOODS RESERVE

Walk through an open eucalyptus forest. Experience the solitude with the trees whispering in the wind. A small dam with reeds adds interest to a classic area of Mornington Peninsula vegetation as it was many years ago.

Start	Gillett Road, Mooroduc South
Distance	5 kilometres return
Time	1 hour 30 minutes plus stops
Effort	Easy to medium
Maps	Melways 152 C5
When	Anytime, except Code Red days

This walk is accessed from near the Camp Niall Scout Camp via Gillette Road. Ample parking is available on a gravel verge.

Head out along the management vehicle track, and listen for the delightful sounds of bell birds. These birds were so loud on a recent visit here that they were clearly audible as I played back the notes from my digital recorder in order to write up this walk. When I did the walk the bellbird calls actually got louder for a short time. I would have to rate this as the best location on the peninsula for bird calls. Come and see what you think.

With such a welcoming greeting the scene was set for a peaceful forest walk. With only one other vehicle parked at the entrance this was not going to be a traffic jam of walkers.

The gravelled management vehicle track is very well maintained and

Woods Reserve.

it would be suitable for strollers with larger all-terrain wheels. There is a fork in the track around 200 metres from the start of the walk. Take the left hand route as the other track heads out to a boundary gate which is visible from the pathway.

Shortly you pass by the dam. This may be the ideal location for a 'cuppa' or snack break on the return journey. A small plastic tarp, two by three metres, makes for an ideal 'picnic ground cover' in such situations.

Keep following the track. There is usually very little wind in a location such as Woods Reserve. The frogs in the dam were making their presence felt. The only thing missing here is the possible inclusion of the picnic table near the dam. This would be a great facility for walkers and families who wish to spend some extended time at this idyllic bush location. Continue walking around the eastern flank of the dam. You will eventually circumnavigate the entire dam.

At the intersection marked with a 'D' post turn left. Some side tracks may be worthy of investigation or perhaps left for another day. There were a number of fallen eucalyptus trees when I last walked at this location and they had been recently sawn to keep the management vehicle track open. The forest appears identical to that seen at the Briars Woodlands and Wetlands Reserve, a few kilometres to the west. The top of the eucalyptus canopy is around 20 metres with substantial thickets of bracken fern. It looks like the country that would harbour kangaroos or wallabies but I have never had the fortune to see one at this location. Continue on the track until you meet up with your original route and then simply retrace your steps back to the entry point.

It would be great to see this reserve and its walking paths linked up with a track that included at least some of the Devil Bend Reservoir.

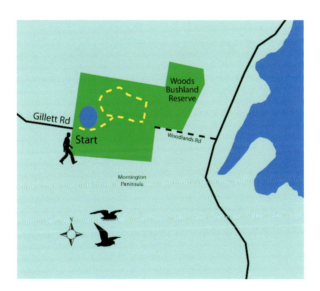

WOOLLEYS BEACH
CRIB POINT

A quieter part of Westernport Bay awaits the keen walker who has a sense of adventure. This track skirts Woolleys Beach and takes you through Woolleys Beach Reserve towards Crib Point. Come off the 'beaten track' to a path 'less trravelled'.

Start	The Esplanade, Crib Point
Distance	5 kilometres return
Time	1 hour 30 minutes
Effort	Easy, flat
Maps	Melways 165 E10
When	Anytime

At the parking area adjacent to the Crib Point Jetty there is a barbecue and an amenities block. The beach here is sandy and there are delightful eucalypt trees to be found along the fringes of this foreshore.

The walk commences by picking up the well formed path which heads roughly south and passes the boat ramp. The boat ramp is about 400 metres distant and there are picnic tables and another barbecue area.

While this area seems somewhat forlorn with a port facility that has fallen into disuse, at the same time this is a very peaceful and serene location. The walker can gaze out over the bay, listening to the crackling sounds of the crabs at low tide, whose homes lie beneath the mudflats here. The calm coastal waters contribute to the sense of a location 'lost in time'. There is a definite feel of being 'away from the rush and the crowds.' This is a relaxing location. It's perhaps reminiscent of

Woolleys Beach.

walking venues of yesteryear, somewhat under-developed, not heavily frequented and awaiting the next 'goldrush' or influx of visitors to liven things up.

From the boat ramp there is another track, presently less well maintained and more sandy in nature, but wide and navigable enough for easy walking. This heads out towards Stony Point along the foreshore. This track meets Stony Point approximately one kilometre from the Stony Point railway station. The track actually meets the road adjacent to an illuminated navigational beacon which is easy to locate. Wildflowers will be in abundance here at the appropriate times of the year.

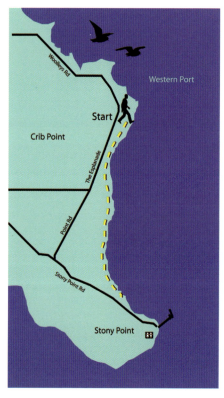

Walking along this track from the boat ramp to Stony Point Road will present little difficulty, the path being flat with a relatively smooth surface. From time to time, you will notice small side tracks to your right. These take you out to the main road, The Esplanade. I decided to turn around when I met up with the Stony Point Road. It would be a fairly uninteresting walk to take the main road to Stony Point. In time, with further track and facility improvements this walk could become a great attraction for the area. A boardwalk from Stony Point to the navigational beacon, similar to the Jacks Beach boardwalk, would give this walk a definite start and end point and highlight the diversity of vegetation around this part of Westernport Bay.

ABOUT THE AUTHOR

Ken's first association with the peninsula was with Safety Beach when he was a boy. Diving and swimming over the summer months. By Year 10, Ken had been camping at Point Leo with school friends during the school vacation.

Later, in his teenage years he would visit Cape Schanck and Fingal Beach where he camped, surfed and walked. Later, visits to Rye, diving and Gunnamatta, surfing, were the order of the day.

Ken's first attempt at writing walking guides was prompted by Flinders Islander (Tasmania) Thelma Shaik who had suggested leaving some notes for guests at her 'Oakridge' holiday accommodation at the village of Killiecrankie, located at the northern end of Flinders Island, Tasmania. The early walking notes were typed sheets placed in a display folder with hand drawn maps added later. The 'Walks of Killiecrankie and Environs' was printed in South Australia in 1997. Later, a walks book for Flinders Island was produced, initially covering 30 locations. The success of this small publication led to the 'at home' publication of the first 'Walks of the Mornington Peninsula' in the 1990's.

Finally, this updated walking guide, produced by **BAS Publishing**, is a continuation of many years association with the Mornington Peninsula. Sam Basile and Ben Graham have both been instrumental in getting this professional publication to press. The author would again like to personally thank Sam and Jean Basile for their great coffees, generosity and commitment in getting this edition to print. Thanks also to Jean Basile for proof reading. Ben Graham has again played a key role in putting this book into the appealing format you now see before you. Rocky has also been another key player in getting the maps together and updating the new walks locations. Thanks also to Charlotte George for the use of her painting 'Pulpit Rock'. Thanks to Peter Skilton and the Mornington Peninsula Astronomical Society for the use of the image: 'Southern Aurora'. Thanks also to Duncan Mather for the initial proofreading. The 'Walks of the Mornington Peninsula' has been the first in a series of five books which are being continuously upgraded and comprehensively revised. This edition of the *Walks of the Mornington Peninsula (2012)* is the fourth print run for this title with a total of 10,000 copies to date. People obviously like to walk. Let's all keep walking.

IN LOVING MEMORY OF MICK MANN

27 February 1960 – 3 June 2011

YOU CAUGHT THE BIG WAVE FAR TOO EARLY

Husband to Jenny, father to Josh, Sam and Sarah

Educator and teacher:
Assistant Principal Rosebud Secondary College

President and Surf lifesaver at Sorrento Surf Life Saving Club

Surfer and a great friend to many

One of Mick's favourite walks was along Rye Ocean Beach

'For you there'll be no more crying
For you the sun will be shining.'
Songbird: Fleetwood Mac

ALSO AVAILABLE

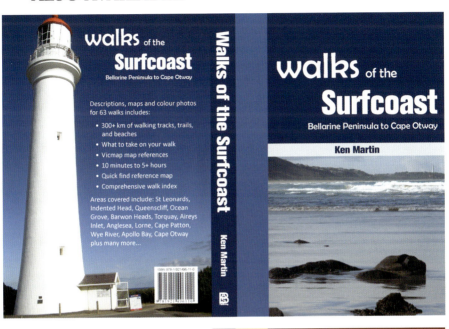

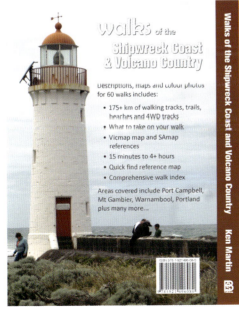

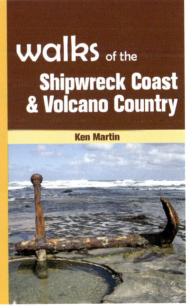

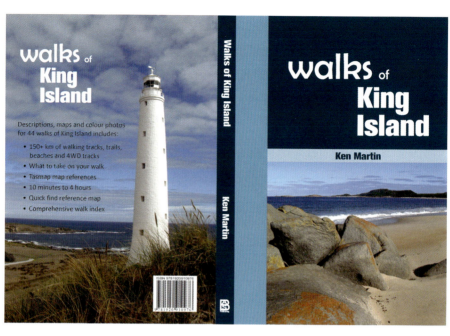

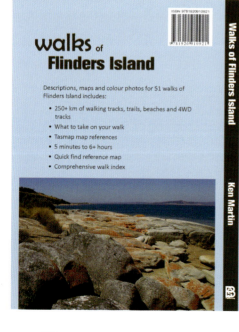
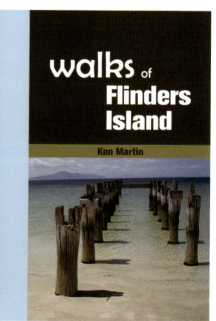

REFERENCES AND RESOURCES

A Field Guide to Coastal Moonah Woodland in Victoria

Australia's Seashores. A.J. Underwood P.A. Hutchings

Australia's Southern Shores. H. Breidahl

Canadian Centre for Occupational Health and Safety 1997-2011

Dogs and Leashes, Birds and Beaches – Birds Australia

Hiking: The Essential Guide to Equipment and Techniques. J. Marais

Holiday magazine. Various issues. A very useful guide to 'what's on.'

Lime, Land Leisure. C. Hollinshed, E. Bird, N. Goss

Melbourne's Mornington Peninsula: Victoria Australia CD

Mornington Peninsula Bathed in Colour. A. Monteith B. Dunkley

Official Guide for Visitors. Mornington Peninsula

Park and Forest Closures on Code Red Fire Danger Rating Days

Park Discovery: Enjoying Victoria's amazing Parks 2011

Park Notes: Various: Parks Victoria

Peninsula Visitor: April – October 2011

Port Phillip Bay. C & M Kerr

Royalauto Magazine: various

Shipwreck Strait. J. Loney

Southern Peninsula News: various

The Age Newspaper: various articles

The Balcombe Estuary Reserve: pamphlet

The Users Guide to the Australian Coast. G. Laughlin

W.J. Dakin's Australian Seashores. Fully revised by I. Bennett

Whale Watching In Australia and New Zealand. P. Gill and C. Burke

Who What Where 2010/2011 The Local Guide

Wind Waves and Weather. Victorian Waters. Bureau of Meteorology

USEFUL WEBSITES

www.parkweb.vic.gov.au

www.parkweb.vic.gov.au/resources/23_2653.pdf
for notification of works within the Mornington Peninsula National Park

http://www.bom.gov.au/products/IDR021.loop.shtml
for the benefits of walking.

http:/www.maps.google.com.au
Google Maps and satellite imagery are also a great resource for the keen walker.